W9-BAC-738

DADDITUDE

DADDITUDE

How a Real Man
Became a Real Dad

Philip Lerman

Da Capo

LIFE LONG

A Member of the
Perseus Books Group

Many of the designations used by manufacturers and
sellers to distinguish their products are claimed as trademarks.
Where those designations appear in this book and
Da Capo Press was aware of a trademark claim, those
designations have been printed with initial capital letters.

Copyright © 2007 by Philip Lerman

All rights reserved. No part of this publication may be
reproduced, stored in a retrieval system, or transmitted, in any
form or by any means, electronic, mechanical, photocopying,
recording, or otherwise, without the prior written permission of
the publisher. Printed in the United States of America.

Designed by Trish Wilkinson
Set in 11-point Garamond by The Perseus Books Group

Library of Congress Cataloging-in-Publication Data

Lerman, Philip.
    Dadditude : how a real man became a real dad / Philip Lerman.
        p.   cm.
    ISBN-13: 978-0-7382-1100-8
    ISBN-10: 0-7382-1100-1
    1. Lerman, Philip. 2. Fatherhood—United States. 3. Fathers—
United States—Biography. 4. Father and child—United States—Case
studies. I. Title.
HQ756.L45 2007
306.874'20973—dc22
[B]   2006038488

Published by Da Capo Press
A Member of the Perseus Books Group
http://www.dacapopress.com

Da Capo Press books are available at special discounts for bulk
purchases in the U.S. by corporations, institutions, and other
organizations. For more information, please contact the Special Markets
Department at the Perseus Books Group, 11 Cambridge Center,
Cambridge, MA 02142, or call (800) 255-1514 or (617) 252-5298, or
e-mail special.markets@perseusbooks.com.

1 2 3 4 5 6 7 8 9

For Harold Lerman

Contents

Acknowledgments

My thanks to the village that helped me bring this about: To Judith Horstman and Jennifer Basye Sander, for getting the ball rolling. Enormous thanks to Jeff Kleinman at Folio, for guidance and wisdom, and to Marnie Cochran at Da Capo, for believing; without you two, it wouldn't have happened. To Carol Weston, for making this so much better. To Amy Eisman and Lydia Strohl, for smart suggestions, and to all who were kind enough to take the time to read the manuscript and offer words of support. Dads need that a lot more than we admit.

I am always and will always be grateful to John Walsh and Lance Heflin, for giving me so many opportunities, without which the opportunity to go off and write this book would never have been possible.

Thanks to cousin Howie, for sage counsel and great humor, and for reading my self-indulgent e-mails way back when and somehow seeing that there might be a book hiding behind them. And to Eleanor, who first taught me to read, and later taught me to want to write.

Mostly, of course, I am grateful to Anna and to Rachel, for teaching me that all you need is love. And patience. Lots of patience. And humor, and determination, and a few other things. But love, mostly.

And to Max, my companion and collaborator, for so many new mornings.

1

Defending the Cavedad

I firmly believe, now that I have quit my job to spend time with one, that I had never before, in my entire life, actually seen a three-year-old.

I've seen many children, of course. How could you not? They're everywhere. But I have uncovered a conspiracy, deep and inbred, which anyone contemplating parenthood needs to know about—especially those who are not only thinking about becoming parents, but who themselves are old enough to be lovingly referred to by my Aunt Dottie as "alte kockers" (old shits).

It's only fair that I tell you about it.

When children turn three, they not only develop the true ability to reason, but at the same time the true ability to refuse to. It's a moment in time when ideas jump out of their heads like fresh popcorn, a moment when they can first identify their favorite color, their favorite food, their favorite Beatle (in my son Max's case, it was orange, whipped cream, and Paul).

It is a moment in time when the true grace of their existence merges with the inherent humor in their perception of the universe. The purity, for example, of Max's need to understand the difference between Indy cars, Formula 1 cars, stock cars, and dragsters (something I had to rush upstairs to check out on the Internet—it's way too soon for him to learn that Daddy doesn't know everything) is as strong as his need to know why cars don't poop. The fact that he can greet the information I provide as though he had visited with the Oracle, and that he seals the bond between seeker and seer with a spontaneous hug, is heartbreakingly wonderful.

It is unfortunate that, at the same time that children reach this state of grace, they go absolutely, undeniably, exhaustingly, bonkers.

And thereby lies the conspiracy. It turns out that people let you see babies when they're cute and cuddly, and toddlers when they're learning to walk, and then—when the child turns three, and goes completely insane—they stash them away for about a year.

My lovely wife, Rachel, who got me into all this, has an explanation for the hide-the-three-year-old phenomenon. To make sense of it, I'll have to give you a little background first. Rachel is a science writer specializing in sociobiology, the belief that much of our behavior is genetically programmed. The sociobiologist's favorite textbook is *Everything I Need To Know I Learned In A Cave*. Sociobiology theory includes many very useful tenets for the average Dad trying to make his way in the world. My favorite—I promise, my wife taught me this—is that men are genetically predisposed to cheat on their wives, while women are genetically predisposed to be faithful.

Now, if anyone is raising a hand at this point to say, "Excuse me, I thought this was supposed to be a book for dads, especially older dads, teaching them how to cope with parenthood, explaining why dads are really more sensitive than Moms, and illustrating how to survive living with a three-year-old. Why on earth would it be relevant, at this early juncture, right here on page three, to discuss the controversial theory that men are predisposed to cheat on their wives?"—to this I would say, Excuse me madam. This is between us boys.

OK. Is she gone? Good. Here's the deal, men. We'll get to the hide-the-three-year-old phenomenon and all the other baby stuff in a minute. But you really need to know this if you're gonna survive parenthood. In fact, if you can make this argument convincingly, the rest will come easy.

Imagine, back in the caveman days, there were two kinds of guys. Those who had the Sleeparound Gene, and those who didn't. Guy with the SG sleeps with, say, three hundred women a year. (Admit it, we all tried to hang around that guy when we were single. He'd have three women around him at the bar, and we'd take the leftovers.)

OK. So let's say SG guy bats a solid .333 and has a hundred kids that year. Meanwhile, Faithful Man—let's call him, for the purpose of this conversation, Alan Alda—has one kid. And one the next year, and one the year after that.

Fast forward a generation. SG's thousand kids and Alan Alda's twelve wimps are out hunting. Which tribe do you think is gonna come home with the mastodon? Now jump ahead another ten generations. Twenty. A thousand. By now, all males carry the Sleeparound Gene; Alan Alda's been bred out of existence along with gills, tail feathers, and back hair (although, if we're really being honest, I have to admit that that last one seems to be taking a little longer for some of us).

My point is this: 100,000 years down the road, we're all bred to cheat, just like Labs are bred to retrieve and basset hounds are bred to slobber on the couch. That doesn't mean we will cheat, should cheat, or have cheated—it just means that when you have the urge to look at other women, you're not being cruel to your mate, just true to your heritage.

Women, it's just the opposite. Let's say there's a woman who's genetically predisposed to sleep with every man she sees. First question: Do you have her phone number? Second question: How many children a year could she have? One, obviously. Same as the Faithful Woman. But the Faithful Woman (let's call her, for the purpose of this conversation, Alan Alda) has a man who stays around to help her ward off the wolves, while the Slut just has a lot of notes carved into rocks saying I'll call you next week. Sure, she could throw those rocks at the wolves, but have you ever seen a woman throw? Clearly the best strategy for women is to be Faithful. Especially to wonderful men like us, of course.

Can you believe my wife taught me this? So, when you're wondering what gives me the authority to give advice on child rearing, just think to yourself: This guy is lucky enough to have found a woman who thinks it's natural for men to be dogs; he must know something. I'll listen for a few more pages.

Good for you! Accepting the fact that Everyone Knows More Than You Do is the first lesson of Fatherhood.

Here is the second. And the most important.

Not too long ago, as Max and I were walking down a busy city street on a sunny afternoon, we passed a parked car with Junior Wells's "Shaky Ground" wafting out the window. A look of wide-eyed wonder broke over Max's face and he started dancing up the street. "Dance wif me Daddy," he insisted.

At the time, I was the co-executive producer of the toughest tough-guy show in the nation, *America's Most Wanted*. I'd picked up Max after a very serious lunch meeting with the FBI (and how strange is it, for an ex-hippie who spent half his life running from the FBI to spend the second half meeting them for lunch?), so I was not exactly in the mindset to boogaloo down Broadway. In fact, even for the ex-hippie-type dad, it's not easy for a fifty-year-old overweight balding white guy to break into dance on a crowded downtown street. Ever. It's not something you like to admit—but there it is. We're just not street dancers anymore.

And then I had one of those Proustian moments (I think it was Proustian, anyway. I know about the madeleines and all, but let's face it, even among us English majors, no one actually ever read Proust. I did finally eat a madeleine, however. Didn't do anything for me)—so, it was one of those if-I-had-read-Proust-I'd-know-if-this-was-really-a-Proustian-moment-or-just-an-acid-flashback moments . . .

. . . and suddenly I was four years old, and skipping down the street with my father.

It was on 212th Street in the Bronx, around the corner from DeKalb Avenue, where we lived; the light was that superreal, late-afternoon, slanting yellow light that exists only in New York, the sidewalk warm from the afternoon sun, the shadows long and soft-edged, the air sweet with the summer smell of baseball-card bubble gum, and I was hand-in-hand with my dad, skipping down the hill from the El-train tracks where the Number Four ran, and my father, in the fedora he wore even with short sleeves in summertime, was skipping too, until some woman appeared from around the corner, and my father suddenly stopped skipping. I insisted that he continue, I implored him—somehow, it was essential to my four-year-old world that we not stop just because people were looking—but he would not abide. He walked slowly and nodded hello to the woman, and after she passed, he began skipping again, but my heart wasn't in it anymore, and as we turned the corner from the bright sunlight into the dark shade of DeKalb Avenue, something was lost that I would never get back.

Until this moment.

So there we are, me in a suit, Max in jeans and a T-shirt, and Junior Wells in a blue Camaro, and Max is pleading with me to start dancing. . . .

. . . and so we do, long-stepping up the street like two stoners in an old R. Crumb comic, and for as many times as you've listened to Martha Reeves and the Vandellas sing "Dancing in the Street" on your oldies station in the last forty years, who else but a three-year-old could actually get you doing it, in broad daylight, on a Tuesday afternoon, in front of people wearing actual shoes and ties? When a child turns three, he becomes a unique sprite, an indomitable spirit, capable of teaching you, like no one else can, that summer's here and the time is right for dancing in the streets. (By the way, did you ever wonder what a "Vandella" is? Turns out Martha Reeves, who was a secretary at Motown Records but got called in to record a single because Mary Wells didn't show up for a session, made up the name. It's a combination of Van Dyke Street, near her home in Detroit, and a tribute to her idol and fellow Detroit singer Della Reese. Van-Della. I didn't know that.) How I came to learn this lesson—the lesson of how to truly give up your dignity and your sense of control, how to truly see the world through the eyes of your child—is the central theme of this book. Or maybe it's a little left of central. The central theme is how Real Men get turned into Real Dads—and once they're there, why they're so good at it (and how they just might survive it).

Because let's face it. If you're a new parent, there's going to be a time when you and your wife are pushing the stroller at one of those stores with ridiculous names like Buy Buy Baby or Toddleknockers or Cutsie Pootsies, or at the drugstore waiting for some perky cashier to get the code for the Suburban Subdivision Size package of Pampers, and you both look bedraggled since you've been up all night for the last three nights because the only way the baby will sleep is if you're walking the floor singing "Baby Love" (by the way, never sing your baby a song you really like: All dads are tempted to do that. But let's say you sing "Happy Together" to your baby one night, and it makes her stop crying. You and your wife will develop a religious belief in The Power Of That Song. So now, in the Who Gets Up With The Baby game, you're suddenly the patsy, because every time the baby cries, your wife will say, "Honey, go in and sing 'Happy Together.'" And it may seem sweet to sing to your little love bundle, "Me and you, and you and me, no matter how they tossed the dice, it had to be"—but trust me, on your four hundredth time through, at four in the morning, you will curse the fact that The Turtles were ever born. On the other hand, did you ever hear Frank Zappa's version of that? It's on the "Live at the Fillmore" album. Turns out Mark Volman and Howard Kaylan, the founders of The Turtles, played with Zappa in the Mothers of Invention for awhile, and for fun they all sang it together in concert. After Frank Zappa was attacked in England by the irate boyfriend of a fan, the band stopped touring for awhile, and Volman and Kaylan left to become Flo and Eddie. I always thought Flo was a woman, but Flo was actually Mark Volman. It's from his goofy Summer of Love nickname, the Phlorescent Leech. Phlo became Flo. See, that's the other advantage of a book just for guys. We know that we like to talk about these things, because they are important. Like what's a Vandella. Women call these unnecessary diversions, and think we talk about them just to avoid talking about other stuff—like, say, what we're feeling. But really, isn't it fascinating to know that the background vocals on Bruce Springsteen's "Hungry Heart" are really done by the original "Happy Together" guys Flo and Eddie? I bet you didn't know that).

So there you are, both looking all bedraggled and stringy-haired in the drugstore, and your wife has that parent-badge of dried baby cheese-up on her T-shirt just above her left boob, and you chuckle for a second until you realize that you do too, and what little hair you have looks like someone put a Brillo pad through a blender, and you look over and see some Fabulous Couple on a Fabulous Date, the kind of dates you used to go on, with women in short black skirts, buying a pack of cigarettes—oh, God, remember cigarettes? Don't get me started on all the terribly healthy things we have to do just because we have kids. Once, I fell asleep in the backseat of a car on the way to New York City, and when I woke up I realized my friend's four-year-old, sitting in a car seat next to me, had reached into my shirt pocket and pulled out a Camel Light and was EATING it, and even that didn't get me to quit, but one look at my little boy's eyes and the smokes were gone forever (well, I still sneak one when his mom's out of town, but that doesn't count)— so the Fabulous Couple is buying their Marlboro Lights, and she tosses her impossibly silky hair back, and in mid-toss she catches your eye for a millisecond and then looks away—and in that millisecond, you wonder, how did I go from that life to this one?

Easy. It's because no one ever showed you a three-year-old.

To understand this, you have to go back to the cave once more. Let's posit that there are two tribes: One is genetically predisposed to take their three-year-olds out in public, and one is not. The tribe that lets young couples see three-year-olds allows them into a spectacle no childless couple is ready for: the unstoppable force, the incredible energy, the astounding stubbornness, the voice that ranges between the decibel level of a jet plane ("your outside voice"), a jack-hammer ("your inside voice"), and the margarita blender at a beach bar ("whispering"). They cannot imagine the unbelievable joy and wonder you feel when you are reading to your child at night, and he falls asleep, tucked safe and secure and peaceful under your arm. They cannot comprehend the sheer exhilaration that a child feels when he knows you are about to tickle him, the open-mouthed, open-hearted glee; or the sheer exhilaration you feel when you finish tickling him and he collapses, giggling and delighted, in your arms, tears streaming down his face from laughter, tears streaming down yours from sheer gratitude for this moment. They cannot comprehend the fact that, for one year, there is a human being who actually believes in his heart that when Daddy kisses a boo-boo, it makes it better. Or, even more unbelievably, that it actually DOES make it better. They cannot fathom your most fervent hope in life, hope that his belief in your healing powers will stay, stay just one more sweet day.

The young childless couple cannot imagine any of this. They can hear only the screeching demand for the most inane things:

"I want to close the door! NO! I WANNA CLOSE IT! YOU CLOSED IT! NOOOOOOO! I WANNA CLOSE IT!"

They see the embarrassed parent trying to quell this hurricane: "Sammy, how do you ask? Can you ask nicely?"

"I WANNA CLOSE THE DOOR! LET ME CLOSE IT NOW! NOW! NOW! (Please.)"

They see the parent, accepting this as a victory, even though he knows, in his heart, that in caveman days there were no doors.

If you have been following the sociobiological argument, which I know you were because it had sex in it, then you will understand that this tribe will clearly die out very soon. Because the young couple, exposed to the vicissitudes of life with a three-year-old, will be much less likely to ever decide to procreate.

They might take up another hobby, which in those days would be, say, hitting rocks with a stick—which is where baseball came from. Baseball was invented by people who decided not to have children, and thus had endless hours to watch other people stand in a field and scratch their private parts. People with children only have a few moments to spare, so they need faster-moving sports. NASCAR is for people with children. You look, you see people driving and taking a lot of left turns, you get it, you can go back in the kitchen and deal with that screaming you just heard, and if there's something good, like a car crash, they'll replay it all day anyway, so you won't miss anything.

Of course, people with three-year-olds do congregate—they just go places with other parents of three-year-olds. It's the leper colony theory. Only those afflicted will enter these gates, along with the occasional missionary (in this world, known as au pairs).

Leper colonies for three-year-olds go by names like Gymboree, or Tiny Stars, or Bouncearama—big rooms filled with colorful mats and gym equipment and swinging ropes and balance beams, all heavily padded like an insane asylum for toddlers, which is exactly what they are. You let thirty or so three-year-olds loose in one of these joints, and it resembles the inside of one of those Electron Accelerator Colliders they spent our money on at college instead of building a new gym.

This is the proving ground that tests the mettle of the older parent, because most of the parents you see are either much younger than you, and eyeing you suspiciously—or they're grandparents, and eyeing you as though you might be one of them. So to prove your true parenthood, you chase around after your toddler as long as you can—in my case, 75 seconds is the going record—and then you collapse on one of the padded couches, shamed by the screech of your toddler across a crowded gym: "DADDY! COME PLAY WITH ME SOME MORE! NO SITTING DOWN! DADDY!!!"

You look at your watch. Thank God. Only one hour until nap time.

Yours, of course. He won't crash for another day and a half.

Those of you raising your hands to ask, "Wait a second, I thought it was the Terrible Twos, not the Terrible Threes"— well, you've hit on one of the great mysteries of life. Namely, where did three-year-olds get enough money to pay a press agent? Clearly, the concept of the Terrible Twos is something created spitefully by three-year-olds, the way Republicans renamed Democrats "tax-and-spend liberals" before creating the biggest budget deficits in history. It's all PR. The Republicans did it via the Fox News Channel (actually, Fox calling itself Fair and Balanced is, in and of itself, a pretty three-year-old view of the world). But I've carefully watched the three-year-old equivalent of the Fox News Channel—it's called *Playhouse Disney*—and it doesn't seem to carry an anti-twoish bias. (Although I did overhear this from a three-year-old on Disney: "Are you twoish? That's OK, some of my best friends are twoish.")

No, the three-year-old's press agency, the one that created the myth of the Terrible Twos, was created like this:

"I NEED A PRESS AGENT! I NEED A PRESS AGENT!"

"No, honey, you can't have a press agent. You're three. That's for grownups."

"I NEED A PRESS AGENT! I NEED A PRESS AGENT! GENERAL SCREAMING! MIND-NUMBING SHRIEKS! EAR-PIERCING WAILS!"

"Now, is that any way to ask?"

"I NEED A PRESS AGENT! I NEED A PRESS AGENT! GENERAL SCREAMING! MIND-NUMBING SHRIEKS! EAR-PIERCING WAILS! (Please.)"

"That's better. OK, we'll sign you up with Dewey Cheatham and Howe."

"NO! DAT TOO DOMESTIC! I NEED MORE INTERNATIONAL EXPOSURE! WAAAAAAA!"

And so, when the rest of us were not paying attention—just like the liberals under Reagan—a New Morning in America dawned, and a new way of looking at the universe was foisted off on an unsuspecting public, and two-year-olds got stuck with the moniker of the "Terrible Twos." So parents of two-year-olds, especially older parents, although stretched to the very limit of their ability to stay awake and run after a toddler, said, you know, this is not so bad. I can handle it. Hey, I'm even pretty good at this!

And then they were three.

For those of you raising your hands to ask, "If it's so difficult for an older parent to raise a three-year-old, why, at the age of 49, did you decide to quit your high-paying job, fire the babysitter, and become a full-time dad?"—Well, my friend, thank you for the exposition and transition, for thereby hangs the tale.

Working at *America's Most Wanted* was the most exhila-
rating job in television. The simple concept—reenact real
crimes, show the photos of the real bad guys, have people
call our hotline with their whereabouts, send cops out to
arrest them, film the grabshot—turned into a national phenomenon. Our successes became quite well-known; what
no one knew was how very hard this show was to produce.

For one thing, we'd be working for three weeks on a seg-
ment about a fugitive and just before we'd air it, the jerk
runs a red light and gets stopped somewhere near Salinas,
and the fingerprints show he's really a murderer on the run,
and the cops call us, and we'd have to pretend that we're
glad the jerk is off the streets, but what we're really thinking, as we take a tape that cost $25,000 to produce and send
it off to the recycling bin, is, why couldn't the fucker have
waited until Monday to get caught, after we aired the damn
piece?

But it's also the most rewarding job I've ever had, and, I
dare say, one of the most rewarding jobs anywhere in television. Now, understand that I'd already had a pretty decent
career in journalism before I showed up at *AMW*—at 24, I
was the city editor of an award-winning small-town paper
and, a decade later, national editor of an upstart unknown
newspaper called *USA Today*—but nothing I'd ever done
came anywhere close to what I was about to experience.

In my very first week at *America's Most Wanted*, a five-
year-old girl went missing. Her family, years later, asked that
we stop using their name, to try to regain some of their privacy, but I can tell you that if you ever watched the show
back then, you would remember the little girl—I will call

her Amy—because she was the most precious, doe-eyed child you can imagine. Her babysitter, a local man in his early twenties, became obsessed with her and, when her mom tried to keep the babysitter away, he freaked out, and kidnapped her.

You cannot imagine what happens to a family when a child goes missing. I could never have imagined. But now, I was their greatest hope. Week after week, I snuck their story onto the air, pretending I had new information (when it was really just some stuff that had gotten left out of the previous week's story). Amy's face was seared in my memory: I saw her everywhere I looked. I lived the case, listened to her mother cry on the phone every day, fretted as the days went by and the local media began losing interest; I found myself walking down the street just thinking of Amy, and I went to sleep at night wondering if we would ever find her.

And then we had a sighting. The babysitter was riding a bicycle east along the Florida panhandle, with the child on the handlebars.

I put their pictures up on a satellite transponder, had my staff call every TV station on the panhandle, begging the stations to take in our feed, run the pictures, help us find this little girl.

And we did.

In those tearful, joyful next hours, as we arranged to bring little Amy back home, as her mother sobbed tears of joy on the phone and I sobbed right along with her, something hardened in me. I became someone who believed: believed in order, in justice, in man's ability to set right what is wrong. It was, until I had a child of my own, the most important thing that had ever happened to me.

By the time my son was born, I'd risen to co-executive producer of the program, which meant I got to argue with our host, John Walsh, about the important victims-rights issues of the day.

Like, how you deliver the line, "You can make a difference."

John had become the host of the show after suffering the most horrible of tragedies: after his son Adam was brutally murdered in 1981, he vowed that his son's death would not be in vain, and he dedicated himself to helping other crime victims find the justice that forever eluded him.

He wanted people to feel empowered, to feel that, working together, we could change the world. He asked us to keep that in mind with every broadcast we produced, and so we decided—he says it was his idea, I say it was mine—to end each broadcast with a signature reflecting that philosophy, while also imploring our audience with a call to action that they could respond to, a plea to become involved.

Only, he says it wrong.

We've had this argument for ten years. John Walsh ends every program by saying, "You CAN make a difference." I told him, over and over, that it was supposed to be "YOU can make a difference." See, his way, the point is that one person is capable of changing the world. We all know that. Look at Mother Teresa. Desmond Tutu. Chuck Berry.

Sure, a person can make a difference—but could *I* be that person? That's another question entirely. I wanted us to answer in the affirmative: Yes. "YOU can make a difference."

Occasionally, John would do a take where he'd read the line my way, but with such an overexaggerated emphasis that it was unusable: "I'm John Walsh. Thanks a lot for watching. And remember—YOUUUUUUUUUUUUUUUUUU can make a difference. There, you happy, Phil?" I actually might have used it on air, but he forgot to walk off screen.

Still, despite these minor squabbles, we did spend fifteen years together, taking more than 800 fugitives off the streets, finding thirty missing children, and getting justice for thousands of crime victims. We were really making a difference. When people asked me how I was able to deal with such violence and death and misery every day, I told them that it was all about focusing on the people who came to us for help, and seeing the difference we were making in their lives. About learning that *I* could make a difference. About living the lesson I'd learned from bringing that little five-year-old girl home: That we can make sense of the universe, bring order out of chaos, bring justice to those who ache for it. I loved my job. I never had a moment's hesitation about what I was doing, and I never flinched—the pain and suffering and torture I was exposed to did not faze me.

That is, until Max was born.

Suddenly, it all became impossible. Producers would come into my office in the mornings, as they always did, and give me the day's news briefing—the murders and mayhem of the night before, the children who were missing but whom we hoped would turn up in the next few hours. And they'd walk out, and I'd be seized with an uncontrollable urge to run home and hug Max.

And one day, I just did.

We'd been working on a reenactment of a drive-by shooting in New York City. A decent, hardworking dad, fresh off the 7-to–3 shift, walking his children home from school, when they crossed through one of those gang disputes that erupts suddenly in gunfire. And the man's seven-year-old son was shot. He scooped up the boy's limp body in his arms, ran into the vestibule of a nearby building, and attempted, in vain, to revive his only son. Our producers had created a touching and painful reenactment of the moment, shot from above, as though from the point of view of the boy's soul, leaving his body, and, as we always did, we had to watch this scene over and over and over, to get the timing just right, to adjust the film look, to make sure the music communicated the horror of the moment without being overdramatized or sensationalistic. Over and over, I felt that boy's soul leave his body. And I sat in the edit room, and I could not hold back the tears.

And over the next few days, with the music adjusted and the scene slightly shortened, with a few different shots placed in, we watched it again, and then again with John Walsh's voice-overs inserted, and then again with the color corrected. And each time, I began to cry again. And finally, I walked out of the edit room, and down the stairs, and into the parking garage, and I drove home, where Max was in his playroom, splayed out on the blue rug, his head on the ground, looking sideways at the wheels of a car he was rolling back and forth in front of his nose.

He looked at me, and smiled.

I scooped him up in my arms, and softly, started singing to him:

"It doesn't matter where you go, or what you do,
I want to spend each moment of the day with you.

'Cause you started something—can't you see
That ever since we met, you've had a hold on me.
It happens to be true—
I only want to be with you."

(By the way, everybody thinks of that song when they think of Dusty Springfield, but have you ever heard her cover of Van Morrison's "Tupelo Honey"? It's transcendent. Oddly, it contains a verse that isn't in the Morrison version. I've always had a crush on Dusty Springfield. Did you know she was deported from South Africa in the mid-sixties for refusing to sing in front of racially segregated audiences? I didn't know that.)

Over the next weeks, and months, I couldn't get the idea out of my head: I'd look at Max's picture on my desk, and I'd think, I want to spend each moment of the day with you.

But could I really do it?

Sometimes, after an hour or so of chasing around after Max, or after responding to his plaintive cries in the pre dawn hours, I'd think, there's a reason people have children when they're young. It's not just that I don't have the energy for this, which I don't. But I think young people haven't yet developed the belief, largely mistaken, that you can control the world around you. Spending 25 years as a news and television executive creates that illusion. Certainly *America's Most Wanted* is a prime breeding ground for the belief in order and justice, but I think anyone who manages people long enough comes to believe that you can, in fact, organize your own world. I had come to believe that with the proper communication tools, with a good team structure, with the right amount of positive feedback bolstered by patient but firm disciplinary actions when necessary, you can control your environment and the people in it.

A toddler takes that belief, and stuffs cheese balls in its ear.

But being an older father, I came to learn, had its advantages, too. We've learned a thing or two about life, having hung around this long. Once we stopped spending all our money on chasing women, we saved up enough to make things a little easier. And certainly, if I've controlled roving packs of wild producers, I could handle a three-year-old.

So I quit the job.

I came home.

And that's when all the fun began.

2

The Vagina Dialogues

There are moments, as a parent, when you have cause to doubt your very sanity.

Moments, for example, when I have been alone with Max for a few hours, and he has spent the last forty minutes hitting the dog with a lollipop and singing, endlessly—

Itsy bitsy spider, climb up a water spout,
Itsy bitsy spider, climb up a water spout,
Itsy bitsy spider, climb up a water spout,

—and I begin to seriously doubt the existence of intelligent life. You do find yourself fantasizing: What if I've gone crazy? What if my lack of sleep has finally taken my brain down South Street, and I've just made up the rest of the universe, and this is really all there is in the world, me and this short person hitting a dog with a lollipop and singing a meaningless line over and over until my teeth fall out, and by the way will the goddamn rain NEVER come and wash the spider out? This drought can't be good for the economy.

But I must also say that hardly a day goes by that I don't look at Max, in some quieter moment, when he's playing Parking Lot with his cars, in some corner, making them all follow some very complex parking rules that only he understands (I try to help him, but I always manage to put some car in the wrong place—is it that the yellow cars can't be next to the blue ones? No two trucks next to each other? Max won't tell. He just yells at me for doing it wrong, then quietly goes about correcting my errors, putting all the cars in their mysteriously right places)—hardly a day goes by that I don't find myself watching him, in moments like these, and thinking: My Max, my Max, my Max. How incredibly unlikely it was that you would ever arrive to drive me crazy.

For those of you who, like me, are older dads, or for those of you thinking of becoming one, I just want to say: When you read in the media about seventy-year-old guys having babies, or fifty-year-old women popping out twins, and there's a vague implication that it had something to do with meditation, Christian Science, and flaxseed oil—well, trust me, there's a lot they don't tell you about how it all happened.

I'm gonna tell you now.

When you're over 40 and still single, you do a lot of math. I remember doing this one a lot: I need to get married by the time I'm 44, because I know I won't want to have a kid right away, since it'll be fun to sleep with the same person every night and have sex anytime you want (yes, I was still that naïve at 40); but I will want to definitely have a kid by the time I'm 46, because if it's a boy, I don't want to be 60 when he's bar mitzvahed. I don't know why, but that was some obsessive goal.

And another one: Even if I make that deadline, still, the only hope of him getting married before I turn 70 is if he gets married at 23. Not likely, given his father's track record with women, but maybe he'll do it as a rebellion thing.

I just had this unshakable fear, which manifested itself in the image of me at my child's marriage, tottering down the aisle, drooling and hacking, gratefully deaf enough so that I couldn't hear the people muttering, "THAT'S the father? Poor kid. Well, good thing his mother's still in good shape." No, that wasn't for me.

So when I did finally find myself contemplating the diamond rings at Boone and Sons—I was 43-and-a-half (yes, I know, most people stop counting the halves when they're nine, but hey, I was getting desperate)—still just under my deadline, I had all the hopes of being able to walk down that aisle on my own steam, without the aid of a portable oxygen tent.

My beloved, a year older than me, already had a kid—ten years old, at the time of our wedding—but was willing to try again. She cautioned me that for a 45-year-old woman and a 44-year-old man, the odds were certainly not in our favor. But I wasn't worried. As any true ex-hippie does, I believed firmly that lots of sex, coupled with lots of positive thoughts, would accomplish all the wonders of the world. I was sure she'd be pregnant in no time.

When I finally got around to proposing—and by the way, ever wonder how to pick the song that for the rest of your life you're going to have to live with as The Song You Sang

When You Proposed? If there are any single guys reading this (and, pardon me, but what are you doing here? Why don't you see if you can find that woman we chased out a while ago, and see if you can buy her a drink?), I can save you a lot of trouble. The only song that is strong enough to carry the moment but not sappy enough to become a horrible cliché as the years go by ("Yes! He actually sang me 'The Way We Were!' I said yes out of pity. Clearly, he needs my help") is the one I eventually went with: Louis Armstrong's "A Kiss to Build a Dream On." My friend Tony wanted me to propose to Rachel while walking down the street, timing it so that at the moment of truth we would turn a corner, where he would have lights hanging from trees, and the Washington Gay Men's Chorus would pop out of the bushes, singing the song; but at the last minute I thought better of it. You gotta watch yourself in these moments.

After the proposal (to which she said yes, thank God), filled with the bliss of knowing our future (also filled with two bottles of Champagne), we symbolically tossed away the birth control. Sure, the wedding was still many months away, but we clearly weren't getting any younger. So, diaphragm and condoms into the trash can, we ventured bravely into the world of Sex For All The Marbles.

For your whole life, you have sex with the express intent of not getting pregnant. Then, one day, you flip that switch, and you're doing it the way God intended (or so they tell us. I personally believe God had nothing to do with sex. I think it's something we figured out on our own. If you were all-powerful, wouldn't you find a less embarrassing way to continue the species?). My loins afire, my heart ablaze, I knew with all my soul that this would work. How could it not? This is how it's done. I couldn't wait, every day, to try again: It was the best pickup line of my whole life, but one I could never, ever have imagined using before: I'd walk up behind Rachel, after dinner, over the dishes, after we'd put her daughter to bed, and say, "Hey, let's go make a baby."

When, at the end of the month, we had that simple proof that it hadn't worked, I was unfazed. Oh, well. Another 28 days of wild sex. And then, 28 days later, that unmistakable single mark on our pregnancy test, the blue mark of a loser. And again the next month, and the month after that. I thought, for some reason, it would happen on our honeymoon—you can't help yourself, you just believe that romance will carry your soldiers to their destination—but again, nothing.

And so we launched ourselves into a series of events, each of which we referred to as The Strangest Thing We've Ever Done—as we entered the promising, terrifying, and enormously embarrassing world of Baby Science.

The first place they send you is to a doctor's office in a place that's always called something like The Women's Gynecological Center For Fallopian Values—letting men know, right away, that this is not your turf. You may enter; you may or may not be needed. Don't speak too much. This is not your place.

And when an older guy walks in, it's even worse. Worse, because you can tell they're all trying to be terribly extra-nice to you, so as not to frighten you. My wife's gynecologist— you know, I could have gone my whole life without finding out that my wife's gynecologist was the best-looking guy on the planet, and been none the worse for wear. This guy was so cute, *I* wanted to have sex with him. But I put the thought aside as I listened to him explain that At Your Age—a phrase we would hear very, very often—there were several choices. We wanted to go with the least invasive one.

"Fine," he said. "We'll start with the Clomid Challenge."

Immediately, I perked up. I love a good challenge! Men are always turned on by competition.

The Clomid Challenge, as best as I could gather (and believe me, this is tough sledding), is a method for determining the level of something called FSH, the follicle-stimulating hormone that's either supposed to be high or low, because one of those things is good, but whichever it was, Rachel's wasn't.

Which was OK, actually, because that led us to Step Two, my absolute favorite part of the process.

Step Two involved the actual drug Clomid, which made Rachel more fertile—a basic rodeo concept, like letting the bulls loose: The idea is, if there are ten or twelve eggs sliding down the chute, one of the cowboys is more likely to catch a ride. The doctor ordered us to have as much sex as possible on those days. (I still send him a Christmas card.) This practice did lead, of course, to the strangest conversations.

"Honey, remember we're supposed to be having lots of sex today. Can you come home around three? Anna will be at a playdate."

"I have a meeting. Call and see if she can stay for dinner. I can be home and naked by five."

Marking the calendar for sex, by the way, turns out to be great practice for after you have a child. Years after Max was born, on those increasingly rare occasions when we'd get both the kids to bed, and my wife uttered the words that have become the starting bell for amorous pursuit ("Honey, did you lock our bedroom door?"), there was still the question of how to be quiet enough during The Act so that wandering toddlers banging on the door don't ask embarrassing questions ("Daddy, why was Mommy talking to God?").

Fortunately, we were still using the baby monitor—these things are incredibly sensitive; I understand George Bush's people are looking into the legality of having them installed at the Democratic Headquarters—and it would catch the sound of the latch of his bedroom door opening down the hall, so we'd have a moment to collect and compose and dress ourselves while the little feet in the feety-pajamas padded down our hall, at which point I'd shuffle him back to bed, and then rush back to Rachel and try to remember where we left off. I would have only been gone thirty seconds, of course—plenty of time for her to fall fast asleep.

Nights in general, in fact, turn out to be pretty lousy times to try to have sex, after you have children. Mornings, too—what with getting a teenager and a toddler up and off to school, getting them fed and dressed and dealing with the crises of the lost purse and the lost blue race car and the lost eye makeup and the lost green race car and the lost homework and the lost yellow race car—and Mondays and Thursdays are out, because the cleaning lady's here, and Wednesday afternoons, because Anna comes home early from school—it turns out Monday at eleven a.m. and Thursday at four are the only times we have free for sex. We've started putting it on the weekly schedule up on the refrigerator, stuck there with a Dora the Explorer magnet.

But hiding-from-the-child sex is not the same as trying-to-get-pregnant sex. The doctor-ordered canoodling was . . . well, it was great, but it didn't get us any closer to parenthood.

And so the science got stranger.

A new doctor, a new plan of attack. Our next meeting was with a doctor who looked just like Charles Emerson Winchester from *M*A*S*H*, only not quite as humble. He puffed his chest out so far I had to move my chair back, as he explained that it was time, now, for the tests. I assumed, of course—not to place blame, because this is not about blame—that this was all Rachel's fault. I had been involved in a few relationships in college that, while not producing issue, let me know I was indeed, capable, of getting a girl pregnant—and so I knew that if we were having a problem, it was with Rachel's plumbing, not mine. I, of course, being the sensitive man, did not bring this up.

Until the doctor said it was me, not Rachel, he wanted to test.

You do not know the meaning of subtle until you are sitting next to your wife in a doctor's office, trying to raise the question of the other girls you got pregnant, without having your wife shoot you a look that will make what little hair you still have fall out.

"Um, what about my, um, history, in the, um, sense of, um, having no previous history of negative results in the area of fertilization?" Aha! A brilliant formulation!

"Oh, yes," he said, looking over my medical history. "The two girls you got pregnant in college.

"Well," he continued, tactfully, "you're not in college anymore."

This doctor does not get a Christmas card.

The day of The Sperm Test, also known as The Most Embarrassing Day Of Your Life, was very strange. It's odd to be sitting at work, thinking, oh, my, three p.m.! I have to go! I have an appointment to masturbate!

This is not a test most men think they're going to have any problem with. After all, they've been practicing for most of their lives (some more diligently than others). But nothing can prepare you for the experience.

It starts when you walk into the Center for Ovarian/Vaginal Awareness. There are women everywhere, in various stages of pregnant. They are knitting, they are reading magazines like *Modern Vulva* with articles like "How to Decorate Your Uterine Wall" and "Why All Men Are Horrible Dogs, and How to Train Yours." You walk up to an attractive young woman behind a glass counter—why is this woman behind glass? Does she think I'm going to rob the sperm bank?—and utter the inimitable phrase, "I'm here to, um, I, uh, I have to, um, the doctor told me to come here."

No pun intended.

I winced when I realized what I had just said, how horribly callous and shallow and stupid I must have seemed, but the attractive woman pretended not to notice.

"Yes, sperm deposit. You can go right down the hall, first door on your left. Exam Room Three. There's a cup for you in there, make sure you put your name on it. Would you like some magazines?"

Now, I don't know about you. I still need to drive across town to buy a *Playboy*, for fear someone I know will show up just as I'm buying it, and I'll be one of those jerks pointing at the magazine with a ridiculous grin on his face, saying a little too loudly, "Look! Great article! 'Britney Spears Tells All!'"

So the idea of saying to this woman, the acting mayor of Estrogen City, sure, gimme a *Hustler*, a few *Penthouse*s, and, hell, while you're at it, throw in a *Double D Damsels*, wouldja?—the idea has me turning shades of purple I haven't seen since those little Pixie Sticks sugar straws we used to get when we were seven.

As she handed me a shopping bag filled with a few girlie magazines, I cast a furtive glance around the room, accidentally locking eyes with a beautiful woman who is clearly 73 months pregnant but still doing her Pilates, eyeing me with the scorn that will follow me through every step of the process, a look of scorn that says, why, oh why, are men necessary for procreation?

A friend of mine found this process so daunting, he decided to do his job at home, then deliver the sample to the lady behind the glass counter. I contemplated this, but once you've completed that task in the privacy of your bedroom, you have exactly one hour to make the delivery, and you have to keep the sample warm. So there he was, driving around the beltway with a jelly jar filled (and I use the term extremely loosely) with his fatherly fluids, jammed under his right arm. Can you imagine what you'd say if you got stopped by a cop? "What's that in the jar, sir?" "Well, I decided it was a good day to jerk off in a jelly jar and then take my little soldiers for a drive downtown, officer." No, not for me. I was going to brave . . . The Room.

As soon as I entered Exam Room Three, I realized that (a) this was the sort of room I'd never been in before, and (b) it was not meant for male eyes.

It was a Gynecological Exam Room.

Men are able to continue with their marriages, year after year, because they do not have to visualize their wives getting a pelvic exam—but once you've seen that table, you're scarred for life. I stood there, staring at something that looked like the result of a strange acid-induced collaboration between Hugh Hefner and the Marquis de Sade: a table covered with white sheets, at the foot of which were two big metal stirrups, about 20 inches higher than the table. Between and below them—at the Nexus of Truth area, if you get my drift—a group of gray, hard plastic probing devices, impossibly complex, the kind of thing you assume the aliens use to insert their Rectal Probes before returning abducted farmers to Iowa where they can tell their stories on Fox News Channel.

Finally shaking off my horror at the sight of the examination table, I cast my eyes around the room, looking for a place to sit and get in the mood. The décor of the room made this seem impossible. Here, on the wall, was a gigantic naked lady—from the inside. She was a faint pink, but her reproductive organs were all brightly colored, from the blue ovaries to the green fallopian tubes to the shocking fuchsia uterus to the big purple vagina—it was as though Dr. Freud interviewed hundreds of boys and said, "Vat is your vurst nightmare? Ah, goot, goot, we make poster like dat." I mean, really. How am I supposed to do what I'm supposed to do in here, while I'm looking at how close this lady's ovaries are to her islets of Langerhans? I remember guys telling me, when I was a teenager, "Oh, man, did you see Sally? She's not wearing a bra! When she bends down, you can see EVERYTHING!" I wanted to call them up and say, you know what? Everything is not something you actually want to see.

On the opposite wall, another gigantic naked lady—this one extremely pregnant, with the fetus clearly visible through her skin. He had those big translucent eyes, like the fetus at the end of *2001*. What's the big deal that women like to go to the gynecologist's office, get naked, and see pictures of other naked ladies who are semi-opaque?

I found the little cup that was to be my date for the afternoon, moved the little metal folding chair around so it wasn't facing Translucent Lass, sat down, and realized I was still carrying my little white shopping bag.

To complete my utter humiliation, somebody had put the three *Penthouses* and a *Hustler* inside a worn white shopping bag that was decorated with . . . three little pink Teddy Bears carrying baskets of flowers. I felt like I should cover the Teddy Bears' eyes when I pull out the *Hustler Big Boob Bonanza Special Edition*, and, without a great deal of hope, set about the task at hand.

No pun intended.

Somehow, about 20 minutes later, I managed to emerge from the room, having successfully violated the plastic cup, which I handed back to the mayor of Estrogen City, and slunk back home.

A few days later, we were back with Dr. Charles Emerson Winchester. The Fallopian Center For Vagina, Vagina, Vagina sent us back to him. Now, he was lecturing me about my sperm. His chest was puffed up so big, we had to sit in the next room. I was taking notes (it helps not to look in a man's eyes when he's using the word "semen" a lot), but having trouble keeping up: Sperm count, it turns out, is the least of the questions. I was sitting through a lecture on all sorts of things I didn't know I was supposed to be worried about: They don't just test the number of little runners. There are also questions like sperm mobility, sperm motility, morphology, volume, forward progression, rushing yardage, and percentage of third down conversions.

Through all of this, I'm wondering, if this was good news, wouldn't he have told us by now? Is it possible that my boys did not pass the test?

Turns out, when they looked at my little school of fish, they found out I've got an army of C-minus students. They're not there in quantities that reach the preferred level of "Mongol Horde"—on number, I barely scored "Jewish Baseball Hall of Fame" levels. But that, it turns out, wasn't the worst of it. My minnows, it seems, didn't swim right.

In fact, they swam left.

Major Winchester, using the calm terms one employs to tell a four-year-old why goldfish have to die, explained that my guys weren't making forward progress. They were swimming around in circles, like Republicans trying to explain why they're voting against health care.

It is in these moments that your little Inner Puritan comes to the fore. What made my boys stop swimming straight? Was it the acid at Woodstock? Unlikely, since I didn't go to Woodstock. Too many nights practicing for the Sperm Test?

"So it's my fault that we can't get pregnant," I found myself saying to Major Winchester.

"Well, we don't like to use the word 'fault'," he said. Unfortunately, he didn't say what word we should use. So fault became the default.

My fault.

A vast, empty space opened in front of me. A space that was once filled with all those images of my son, or daughter, at all those various ages—images of me cuddling, feeding, cajoling, teaching to throw, walking to school. I knew, at some level, that there were options still ahead; but in that moment, there was only hopelessness. I've always loved it when one of my little nieces, walking next to me down the street, curls all of her little fingers around my index finger. I looked at my index finger now. No part of me ever felt so naked, so alone.

I felt very, very old. I thought of all those women in the waiting room at Estrogen City, popping into the sack for a quickie with their husbands one night, taking their little over-the-counter pregnancy tests, popping out their little babies, and I felt a thousand years older than them, and their husbands, and a million years too old to be a father.

And I started to cry.

Now, my stepdaughter will tell you, because it is one of the great embarrassments of her life, that I am an easy cry. I am guaranteed to cry once in every movie. Even *Caddyshack*. (Well, come on, you have to admit, when Bill Murray does that little soliloquy about the former greenskeeper winning the Masters, that's a pretty emotional moment. Even though while he's doing it, he's knocking the heads off some chrysanthemums with a nine-iron.) Nevertheless, the thought that we not only would never get pregnant, but that I was to blame, was too much to handle.

Major Winchester noticed my tears, and showed his good bedside manner by actually deflating his chest a few inches. He told me that we had many, many options to consider.

My sperm could still fertilize Rachel's eggs—but if they were going to make the long trip up the Fallopian Highway, they were going to need an assist.

Enter the Turkey Baster.

Our best option, it seemed, was for me to go back to Estrogen City, "collect another sample," and have it inserted on Ovulation Day (we had by now turned this into such a major holiday that I started giving my staff the day off with pay). The insertion—basically placing the sperm directly on their target—was done with an instrument known, affectionately, as The Turkey Baster.

This, by the way, was still on the list of Less Intrusive Procedures. Wait. It gets worse.

Now, in order to prepare Rachel for this process, and give my hopeless little boys their best shot at doing what they were born to do, I had to learn something that I could have gone several lifetimes without knowing.

Which is, How To Give Your Wife A Shot In The Butt.

To prepare for Turkey Baster Day, they wanted to make sure that my little handicapped Olympians had as fertile a playing field as possible. So I had to shoot Rachel full of drugs that would make her eggs plentiful and her womb fluffy.

I felt like Farmer Brown, taking courses at the 4-H on how to fatten up a chicken.

On Turkey Day Minus Thirty, we began. I'd done very well on my lessons. You practice, of course, by giving shots to a honeydew melon. That's easy. The hard part is staring at your wife's naked butt under the brightest lights in the house and not telling her how much her butt cheeks do not resemble honeydew melons. I told you, there are many, many pitfalls along the way in this process.

The way I get through it is a particularly Guy way of handling these things, gleaned from watching a thousand sci-fi movies: While you're standing there, your nose two inches from your wife's derrière, the needle poised in the air, you just pretend that it's one minute in the future. Your wife has just said, "Hey, that didn't hurt too much." Now you go back in time one minute, to the moment with the poised needle. You quickly "relive" the moment that has already happened—watching the needle go in "again," quickly, and waiting once again to hear your wife's response.

"Ow, shit! That hurts!" Rachel said.

Hmm. Just like in the sci-fi movies. The act of time travel has altered the present. I hate when that happens.

Over the next few days, I got better at the task. Soon Rachel wasn't complaining much more than the honeydew melons did. I know this all sounds terribly unromantic—staring at your wife's butt under bright lights, talking endlessly about sperm motility and egg timing—but once again, the life-affirming goal of making a baby became an enormous turn-on.

Finally, the big day arrived. By now, I was an old pro at The Jane J. Menstruation Memorial Tampon Center. I strode up to the counter, scooped up my Teddy Bear Bag Of Dirty Magazines, headed off to Exam Room Three—the same room, it turns out, where the "insertion" was scheduled a few hours later—said hello to my translucent lady friends, and went to work. In the end, practice makes perfect.

So that afternoon, I was back at Baby Doc's with Rachel, and we were both nervous. A hundred shots in the tushie were all leading up to this afternoon. The doctor, a skinny man from India, was going to perform the procedure. He asked me if I wanted to be in the room.

Now, here's an ethical dilemma you'd better be prepared for. You know those games the kids play today—the ones that supposedly test your mettle as a human being? "Which is worse—having to bite a cold sore off your dog's tongue, or falling head first into a porta potty?" I'm not sure the point of this game, other than to gross you out (wait—these are teenagers. Of course. That IS the point of the game).

But there I was, smack in the middle of it. Which is worse—watching a skinny guy from India inseminating your wife with a turkey baster, or knowing that, at the moment your child was conceived, you were in another room reading *Cosmopolitan*?

Maybe, if there was better stuff to read in the waiting room, I might have opted for the latter. But for some reason, I flashed on a joke my father told me, at a seminal moment in our lives.

No pun intended.

My father, a failed vaudeville comic, had a gift of timing that was like none other. We were in a hospital in Queens; he was 82, and being wheeled down a hallway on a stretcher, headed for a quadruple bypass operation. We knew, that at his age, there was a chance I'd never see him again. He motioned me down, to put my ear near his lips so I could hear what he had to say. I waited for those meaningful words, perhaps the last I would hear; some declaration of eternal fatherly love, some long-held deep spiritual truth. Here's what I got:

"Guy says to his wife, 'How come you never tell me when you have an orgasm?'

Wife says, 'Cause you're never there.'"

I don't know why, but my father's words—"'cause you're never there"—were ringing in my ears in this moment, and I could not imagine being absent at the moment of conception. I did avert my gaze at the Moment of Truth, staring instead into my wife's lovely hazel-green eyes, imagining the phone call we would get, a few days later.

We went home, and I showed Rachel an *I Love Lucy* episode I'd snared with the TiVo. It's the one where Lucy's husband, Ricky Ricardo, doesn't know she's pregnant, and she keeps trying to tell him, but he's too busy, so she finally manages to tell him while he's on stage at the Club Babalu, and he freaks out, and then he sings to her, sweetly and slowly, "We're Having A Baby (My Baby And Me)."

Turkey Baster or no, it didn't take. Not the next month, either. Or the month after that. A hundred shots in the butt later, and still we faced, again, that dark abyss.

We chose the next step ourselves.

Against all advice of doctors, friends, and pamphlets (be prepared, if you're going to go this route, for pamphlets. Everybody gives you pamphlets. At every Center for Women's Thingies, no matter what question you ask, you get a pamphlet. They all show a happy couple with a baby on the front, and they're written in Very Simple English So That You Can Understand Why We're Charging You Such Ungodly Amounts Of Money)—against everyone's advice, we were following two paths simultaneously.

We were deep into the scientific world of assisted pregnancy—but we were also deep into the world of private adoption.

At our age (boy, you get tired of hearing people, including yourself, start sentences with that phrase), no adoption agency will talk to you. Doesn't matter that we were two loving, financially secure people who could give a child a wonderful home and ridiculous amounts of neurotic attention. Birth moms just don't want to see their babies being adopted by people who look like they could be the baby's grandparents.

And so, with the help of a wonderful group known as Families for Private Adoption, we learned how, on our own, to become legally certified for adoption, to set up a separate "baby line" phone—and how to spread the word, which became the next Strangest Thing I've Ever Done.

It turns out, when you're trying to adopt privately, the strategy is to Tell Everyone. You make up little cards to hand out. Ours said:

"A happy, loving, financially secure couple seeks to adopt an infant. We'll pay legal and medical expenses. Willing to adopt mixed-race baby. Let's help each other. Call Rachel and Phil anytime at this number. Collect calls accepted."

We handed these cards out to everyone: Checkout girls at the grocery. Cleaning ladies. The guy who brings wood around in a truck and insists that a face cord is the same as a full cord (It's not. A cord of wood is eight feet by four feet by four feet, stacked neatly. A face cord less than half of that. A pickup truck holds much less than a full cord. Don't be fooled. But be nice, and give him your adoption card anyway).

We just kept handing out those cards. And one day, just after our third failed Turkey Day, and just a few months into an adoption search that we were assured would probably take a year, we got a call on the Baby Line.

"Hello," my wife heard a breezy teenager's voice say. "Are you the couple that wants a mixed-race baby?"

The next afternoon, we rented a car—never go in your own car, our pamphlet said. Begin planning for anonymity right now—and drove across the river from Washington, DC, where we live, to a pretty crummy part of town in Arlington, Virginia, where we were to meet the teenager and her baby at a Denny's.

It's always a Denny's. Denny's is the official adoption first-meeting place. I don't know why they don't put it in their ads. "Come for a burger—leave with a baby!" It would get my attention.

She breezed in, a pretty, skinny blond girl, the sun through the plate-glass window highlighting a walking mobile of bracelets, piercings, necklaces, and rings, pushing a stroller and chatting with a friend who'd come along for the ride. She sat down, gave us a brief hello, and immediately got to the business of ordering lots of food.

"Would you like to hold Keisha?" she asked me and, without waiting for an answer, performed those quick slip-clip moves parents all seem so deft at, unhooking the baby from the stroller and plopping her on my lap.

Keisha was, I must say, the most beautiful baby I had ever seen. Chubby and mocha-skinned, with impossibly big, dark eyes. She immediately stuck a finger in my beard, and looked at it with a big, drippy, toothless grin. "Hello, young lady," I said to her. "Barra! Barra!" she said to me.

And so it began.

Rachel and the mother chatted, Rachel getting the young girl's story: Her boyfriend had left her. She was living in a $50-a-night room with four other girls and the baby. She couldn't take care of her and keep her job. She needed to work the next night—could we babysit?

I only half-listened to the story. I was absorbed with Keisha. Little Keisha. My little Keisha? One of those strange things that happens when you're married is that you find out about little dreams, now and then, that you didn't know you shared. I'd always imagined adopting a black child, or a mixed-race child. I don't know why; I always assumed it would happen without realizing I was making that assumption, until one day it becomes part of your life plan, like it was always there. Rachel, it turned out, had always felt the same.

And yet, here I was, sitting with a baby on my lap, the child of a blond woman and a black man, a baby clearly not Caucasian by any stretch, and I wondered: Have I really got what it takes? Could I really be the white balding Jewish father of a little black girl? Could I do this?

Now, you may not believe what happened next, but I swear that this is true. I have always, always believed that at key moments in your life, a song will come on the radio that tells you what to do. You are not obligated to carry out its message—you don't want to be Son of Sam about it, I mean, you're trying to figure out what to do about your noisy neighbor, and you hear "Helter Skelter," and suddenly you're Charles Manson; no, you have to be circumspect about this—but I have always believed in the Oracle of the Radio.

So there I am, contemplating this moment, wondering if I could actually cross this threshold, become that guy, already stepfather to a teenager, now adoptive father of a black baby, and, so help me God, Michael Jackson comes on the radio. He is singing a song I have not heard since it was a hit a dozen years back. I couldn't believe it. Could it really be? As the lyric rolled on, my face flushed, and the tears started to flow, as I listened for the line I knew was about to come: When you are talking about your baby, Michael was imploring me, it doesn't matter if she's black or white.

We didn't come to any decision right then and there, other than that we thought Keisha was the most wonderful baby on earth. We finished lunch and agreed to babysit for a night.

Keisha went to sleep so easily that night, and I sat and listened to that tiny, tiny breath in the dark; and the next night, when we had returned her to her mother, and met with our lawyer, and gone home, I suddenly felt miserably alone. Like I had left something terribly, terribly important behind.

Rachel and I went out into the backyard, and stared up into the stars, and I started crying again. "That's our baby," I said to her through the tears. "Let's go get our baby."

It was that simple.

Until the father showed up.

A few days later, after hurried doctor visits and signed forms and a whirlwind of expensive lawyer calls, we had just one task left: to locate the biological father, who had long since left the scene, and get him to sign the adoption papers. You shouldn't do it without his signature, said our lawyer; even though he's left the mom and Keisha months ago, nothing could stop him from showing up five years from now and claiming his child, and nothing in DC law could prevent him from taking the child away from you.

Which is what he decided to do, then and there. He decided that no one was going to call him a bad father—no one was going to raise his child for him. He would do it himself, goddamn it. She could live at his cousin's house. So at three a.m., deep in a moonless Virginia night, he showed up at the fleabag motel, grabbed Keisha, and took her away.

Forever.

I had three long, straightforward, man-to-man conversations with him, by phone, over the next two days. I tried everything in my power, all the persuasiveness I'd learned in 20 years of management, all the ways I knew of making him feel empowered to change his decision. And I almost succeeded.

Almost.

In the end, we had to walk away.

Without Keisha.

For days, I was inconsolable. I had a picture of me with Keisha, and I couldn't stop looking at it.

My sister called at work, on the third day. "You know," she said, "Somewhere out there, a baby is smiling today. Because now that you didn't adopt Keisha, he—or she—gets to be your baby. And he's very, very happy about that. He just has to find his way to you. But he's smiling today."

It was very hard for me to hear, on that day. But I know, now, that she was right.

People say it's like being on a roller coaster, all the ups and downs you go through when you're trying to have a baby, but I think it's a bad analogy. Roller coasters are, at least, thrilling and exciting, and you know you're going to get off them at some point. This was not a thrilling and exciting ride. This was getting to be like a long, painful movie your parents would take you to, when you were little, like *The Sky Above The Mud Below,* which was a documentary study of life among the natives of Dutch New Guinea as witnessed by a group of Gallic explorers, in which the highlights are shots of rare animal species encountered by the natives. Very, very few car chases. Our quest to become parents was like that—endless, repetitious disappointment.

It is also, for a man, gallingly impossible to control. They say that to understand the difference between men and women, present them with a problem. Women will say, "Oh, that's terrible! How do you feel?" whereas men will say, "Oh, that's terrible! Here's what you have to do. Get an Allen wrench. . . ." We are, by gender and nature, problem solvers. Fix-it types. That's why we like action heroes. They get stuff done. We like that. And when you spend half your life managing people, and half of that time solving crimes and putting bad guys behind bars, it's just not in your nature to see a problem and say, this is beyond my control. Even with an Allen wrench.

So, I was not handling this all that well.

Then, one night, there appeared on my pillow an article—a sign from God?—no, wait, Rachel put it there—about donor eggs. Now, of all the Strangest Thing I've Ever Done stuff we'd done, this was the one we'd decided early on we could never do: Find a woman who was ovulating, have her eggs removed, have them fertilized by my dizzy little spinning sper-mies, inserted into Rachel, and—for goodness sakes, who do we see for this, Doctor Orwell?

Then I read a little further. The chances of success for a couple our age were 50 percent on the first try, 75 percent after three tries.

The next morning, we started on our Donor Egg Hunt.

There are two ways to do this (it seems like there are two ways to do everything, when you're trying to have a baby. Door Number One and Door Number Two. But no Monty Hall to offer you a thousand dollars to change your mind). There are the small, friendly clinics, and then there's the Ge-netics and In Vitro Fertilization Clinic, affectionately referred to by all the people who know about these things as The Baby Factory.

At our small, friendly clinic (I think it was The Clitoral Clinic For Get Your Penis Away From Me And Wellness Cen-ter), we found out it would be months before a donor might become available. We were resigned once again to our fate, until we went out to dinner one night with some friends who'd recently moved to New York City. They'd had The Best Looking Baby On The Planet, which was not surprising, since they were Best Looking Couple On The Planet: She was a former model; he was, I think, the guy whose chin they use to carve marble statues of other guys who are not quite as good looking as him. We told them what we were going through, and they looked at each other, and whispered to each other, and turned back to us.

"We haven't told anyone this," they said.

"We haven't even told our parents this," they said.

"Chelsea is a donor-egg baby."

"We found our donor at GIVF."

The Baby Factory!

The model leaned across the table, and put her hand on mine.

"Go there."

Now, when beautiful women lean across the table and put their hands on yours, I don't care how important the conversation, there's only one thing guys think: Uh-oh, did anyone just catch me looking down her shirt? I quickly popped my gaze back up to eye level, figured I had gotten away with it, and tried to remember what we were talking about.

Oh, right! The Baby Factory! Wait—did she just say what I thought she said?

That beautiful baby—doesn't carry her genes?

She's a donor-egg baby?

A few days later, there we were, at The Baby Factory, flipping through page after page of donors. They were all anonymous, of course, but gave their medical histories, along with many other details, some relevant, some as irrelevant as they come. SAT scores; OK. Eye color; I understand that. Favorite movie? Why, just in case you think liking *Flashdance* is genetic?

Most of these women, we were told, were not doing this for the money. They had to go through a lot of testing, screening, and more testing to get to this point. Most of them, we were told, were doing it because they felt it was a good thing to do. God bless them! Little Janie Appleseeds, planting joy in the barren fields of our life. We felt excited and renewed. We started making our decision.

We decided to look first for a Jewish donor, but quickly gave that up. Apparently, Jews don't donate eggs. I don't know why. It's not against the religion. And it's not that we're a particularly selfish people. I think it's just too frightening. I think it was Woody Allen who first noted that when we were teenagers, the rabbi would tell us that every time we masturbated, we were killing a million potential Jews.

I think maybe there's some Holocaust survivor thing that makes us hoard our eggs, so the Nazis won't get them, or something.

Or maybe we're just too neurotic. When it comes to Jews, that's usually a safe place to start the betting.

Most of the women who'd made it through the screening process were top-notch egg donors: Their photos, at three years old, were attached to their forms. They were uniformly adorable, with high SAT scores and, for the most part, very girlish movie choices. (Come on, could anyone's favorite movie really be *Pretty Woman*?) Adorable, that is, except the Jews. There were about four of them, and they all had high school equivalency degrees and looked, even at three years old, like my Grandma Fagel. Who looks, oddly enough, exactly like George Washington. When I first moved to DC, I was struck by the fact that everywhere you went, there were great portraits of my Grandma Fagel, crossing the Delaware, riding a horse, or signing important documents. In one terrifying moment, I came across the great Greek marble statue of George Washington that lives in the basement of the National Museum of American History. The statue looked even

more like Grandma Fagel than the portraits did. The statue
was adorned only in a toga, for some reason, exposing one
of Grandma's boobies, which is not a sight you want tourists
from Arkansas parading past all day. I'm glad it was down in
the basement. The statue's right arm was uplifted, index finger pointed skyward, in a pose I knew all too well. Few
tourists could possibly know what the Father of our Country
was saying at that moment: "Get out of that wet bathing suit,
mine kinder! You'll chafe!"

So we gave up on the Jew thing. We decided to just look
for donors who were smart, and healthy, and cute.

And suddenly, there she was.

Number 619.

The X chromosome we were looking for—the woman
who would become the X in Max.

Here at The Baby Factory, it all went very efficiently:
even the dirty magazines were current. It was just a matter
now of picking the right date, based on the availability of
the donor egg.

Remember how I was saying that each stage involved
The Strangest Thing You've Ever Done?

Well, picture this: Our lives now revolved around the
menstrual cycle of a woman whom we only knew as a picture of a three-year-old girl. It felt vaguely . . . icky, is the
only term that comes to mind. Then, picture this: You are
making your wife's womb artificially soft so that a fertilized
egg from another woman will successfully imbed in it and
grow to maturity. OK, now you understand that we are
reaching new heights on our Strangest scale. But onward
we pressed.

The revelations came in stages: First, that our donor had ovulated, and produced eight eggs; second, that my little dizzy gillespies had managed to merge with five of them; third, that those five had continued to develop, and were ready to implant; next, that the doctors recommended implanting three; and finally—that the implanting had to take place the next day.

Holy shit!

About a week later, we were sitting on a bench in Chautauqua, New York, a lovely little lakeside community where Rachel's mom and dad had a cottage, where Rachel spent every summer of her life. All four of our parents had passed away before we met, so we decided that making the call from her mom's favorite bench would be a nice way of involving them. It was a little stone bench, right by the lake, hidden by a grove of bushes. I never got around to putting The Baby Factory on my speed dial—it's just too prestigious a position in your life, the ten primary speed-dial slots (well, nine, actually, since Verizon is audacious enough to decide that your number-one slot should be saved for speed dialing your own voice mail. I mean, really, who are they to say? First of all, there's already a shortcut for voice mail, which is *86, which is easy to remember because Maxwell Smart was Agent 86. The number "86" itself was a joke, of course, referring to an old term meaning "to cut someone off" or "kick them out of the bar." There are lots of theories of where the term "eighty-six" came from—most of them wrong. The most common is that it came from Chumley's Bar, at 86 Bedford Street in Greenwich Village—a bar with few markings out front and lots of hidden exits out back. So you could easily disappear there, if you wanted to—you could 86 yourself. But the term goes back further than the bar, so 86 that explanation. It's actually one of those terms used by soda jerks back in the '20s, like "Adam and Eve on a raft" were poached eggs on toast. To 86 an order was to cancel it. The number "86" was picked, probably, because it rhymed with "nix"—or maybe the numbers they assigned were just random. Guess what the number was for the boss? It was 99. That's why Barbara Feldon became Agent 99. Man, she was so hot.).

Rachel convinced me to put aside further explanations of why GIVF wasn't on the speed-dial, and to make the most important call of our lives.

It had been such a long, and complicated, and heart-wrenching process to get here.

And such a simple ending.

Rachel was pregnant.

3

Waiting for the Miracle

There are two things that usually go along with being an older parent.

One is, you have to get used to a house littered with reading glasses and pacifiers.

The other thing is, one of you has probably been down this road before.

With us, Rachel was the one with a kid. Anna, eight years old when I met her, was the most energetic and astounding being I'd ever met. She is a testament to why people love people with attention deficit disorder (ADD). Now, before I go on, I should mention that my lovely stepdaughter, my lovely wife, and my lovely boss at *America's Most Wanted* all have attention-deficit disorder, so I consider myself an expert on the matter, and I can tell you this: the disorder has nothing to do with a deficit of attention. In fact, ADD people are the most attentive in the world: When they're locked in on something, the house could be burning down around them, and they wouldn't notice. That's why the rest of us love them: When you're talking to them, they make you feel like you're the only person in the universe. This, by the way, was Bill Clinton's secret. He didn't have ADD, but when he talked to you, he acted like he did.

Anna and I would make up secret languages (secret because they were actually gibberish, but we'd pretend to have very long and serious conversations in them. She could keep this up forever); or we'd invent silly games (the Beatles dolls I gave her became crazed, incompetent aliens on a mission to steal the shoes of Anna's American Girl doll, for example). She would focus in so thoroughly, so completely on these games, that I could not help but get swept away into them, and into the joy of being with someone with such a capacity for happiness.

People with ADD, however, also sometimes tend to be hyperactive, which Anna most certainly was, as well. In the first five minutes of our first meeting, she had sung me a song, interviewed me on videotape, shown me most of her toys, and, if I'm not mistaken, picked my pocket. This was a kid who was going places.

So when older people have kids, you tend to have these big age ranges in the house, along with big personality ranges—in my case, today, living with three people, one of whom is going through puberty, one through toddlerhood, and one through menopause.

We have a dog so obsessed with chasing balls that she once, literally, ran the pads off the bottoms of her paws. And she's the calmest one in the bunch.

The decision that brought us to this new place at this late age, the decision to have a baby—leaving us with a teenager and a toddler at the same time—was based on a single not-so-well-thought-out-premise:

Hey, I know! Let's NEVER SLEEP AGAIN!

These days, it's around 7:30 in the evening when I say to my lovely bride, hey, let's get Max to sleep on time, and watch a movie. It's around 7:30 and ten seconds that she says, "Sure thing, hon!" with that look on her face that says, "And what planet did you just arrive from?"

It's around 8:30 by the time Max has taken his bath, brushed his teeth, run around the house naked shouting "Everything is everything!"—actually, quite an enjoyable experience, you should try it sometime—been forced into his pajamas with the use of bribery, cajolery, threats, and physical restraints (if you manage to pull the pajama top over their heads, for God's sake, never put their arms through the sleeves! It works like a straitjacket for just long enough to get pants off, skin ointments applied, and pajama bottoms in place, if you go really fast and work as a team. Any two parents who have dressed a three-year-old for bed are immediately qualified to work on the pit crew at Daytona—actually, that would be the easier task, because when you're changing his tires, Michael Waltrip is less likely to be flapping his arms, jumping on you, and yelling, "I a bird! I a bird! I fly now! Wheee! I land on your head!" Well, actually, they are thinking of adding that to the NASCAR circuit, but it's still in the talking stages).

So it's about 8:30 when we've gotten Max into bed, and 9 by the time we've finished reading books to him (at four years old, you can't cheat anymore. I used to get in and out of reading time in about five minutes, by skipping pages. "A little bird was looking for his mother. He found her. The end." Now, Max notices if I skip a single word. "The little ducks waddled home to their mother." "No, Daddy,

the little ducks waddled QUICKLY home to their mother."
Four years old, and he's a purist for the unabridged *Quackie
the Duck*). At 9:01, Anna suddenly needs to be driven back
to school, where she left a book that is ESSENTIAL for studying for a test tomorrow. We go, and are back home at 9:45.
At 9:46, she announces that she is done studying, and needs
a ride to Andrew's house.

OK, 10 o'clock. Still time for a movie. No, wait! Max is crying. He had a bad dream. Something, not surprisingly, about
ducks. At four years old, Max is convinced that Daddy has to
come chase the bad dreams away.

May he never stop believing that, and may I always believe I can.

Movie time is ticking away. Now Rachel's on the phone
with Anna. It's 10:45; Anna wants to stay out until midnight,
because Andrew's friend is bringing over some Really Cool
Thing (musical instrument, unrated DVD, computer soft-
ware, junk food from Wisconsin, guy he met at camp, girl
who knows Fiona Apple, tape of a *Family Guy* episode
they all have to watch together). Rachel is saying no. At 11,
Rachel is still saying no. At 11:15, Rachel is still saying no.

Having stuck firmly to her guns, Rachel finally goes to
pick Anna up. They get home at midnight.

Just in time for Max to wake up again. Water.

12:15–12:20: Arguing with Anna about getting off the
computer and going to sleep.

12:45–12:50: Ditto.

1 a.m.: Max. Water AND ducks.

2 a.m.: Rachel, hot flashes.

Finally, finally, finally, around 2:30 a.m., I sit up in bed,
and listen to the soft whoosh of the air conditioner, realizing:

It is finally quiet. All my little ducks are asleep. I fluff my pillows, tuck myself under the covers, spoon myself up to my wonderful, warm, ever-so-slightly snoring spouse, and close my eyes, ready to drift off to a deep, well-deserved rest.

That's when the dog throws up on the bedroom rug.

It is in these early-morning hours, settling into the task at hand with bucket and paper towels and AFTA dry cleaning spray, knowing that at best I have two hours before it's time for Max to wake me up again, that I realize how much better suited I would have been to this task had it only occurred to me to take it on 20 years earlier, when I had hair and stamina and an unblinking faith in the notion that tomorrow will be different. It is that mixture of youthful exuberance, youthful energy, and youthful stupidity that gets regular parents through; a mix that, now, sadly, was gone, along with my ability to snort coke, smoke dope, eat chili, drink rum, screw until dawn, and still show up for work with the ability to keep my head off the keyboard.

Yes, scrubbing away, getting just a slight high from the fumes of the dry cleaning spray, already bleary from the long, long road to slumberland, your youth feels like a distant memory, gone with the wind, and it becomes very clear why people do this (have babies, that is, not clean up dog vomit) at a much younger age than you.

It's something we were reminded of all through Rachel's pregnancy—never so clearly as in Baby School.

Baby School is the great equalizer. Everybody gets put together not by class, race, age, Red State, Blue State; it's just the totally random chance of how pregnant your wife is. So we had a nice rainbow coalition of preggos and their mates—even one lesbian couple. All shapes and sizes, a nice bell curve of humanity.

And then, way, way off to the right of the bell curve (imagine the little head of a snake with an elephant in his belly)—there were me and Rachel. Old enough to be everybody's mother and father.

To make matters worse, everyone in these classes is very Sincere. Straightforward. Listening Very Carefully. Which, I guess, makes sense, given that this is the most important thing you're ever going to do and all. But you realize that people in their 20s still have a tolerance for being talked to like children, since it's not that far off for them. The teacher is mumbling something about, "Now, for relaxation, we like to think of some place that makes us happy. Do you have a place that makes you happy?" And the preggos and their mates are saying, "The beach," "the country," "a green field with butterflies" (I swear. I wrote it down)—and I'm thinking, yeah, I have a place that makes me happy. A room with none of you in it.

As far as I could tell, the main goals of this class were two:

- Give you confidence and relaxation techniques, so you can approach the birthing process without fear.
- Scare the shit out of you.

Max was still a month away as we were wrapping up birthing class. I had lived through the worst of it—the early months of pregnancy, when we first saw Max inside Rachel, and those scary sonograms that followed, as we peeked into his room to make sure he was OK (my friend Sharon married a gynecologist in Las Vegas, and we flew out for the wedding, and he threw in a free sonogram as a party gift); the scary progression, first a grain of rice with a heartbeat, to an impossibly fragile-looking fetus waving at us (or was it thumbing his nose? I wasn't sure), those early months when we knew the chances of him surviving, because of his lineage and Rachel's age, were not terrific—to now, when we knew we were in the home stretch.

In the home stretch, and sitting with these babies having babies, learning all the things that could still go wrong during birth. The umbilical cord could get wrapped around his neck. The placenta could go sour. Terrorists could bomb the hospital (This technically had nothing to do with the birthing process, but after 9/11, you started thinking this way). I had a friend at work who lost a baby at 38 weeks—I could not even imagine the unbearable pain; he was writing a book about it, and asked me to read the rough manuscript. I could not even keep it in the house. I put it in the garage, hidden away. I didn't even like to look at it.

Because a part of me knew that, at my age, at Rachel's age, this might be our last shot. This is the true essence of having a baby as you're approaching 50—the knowledge that you might never get another chance. The doctors knew it, too. Their euphemism for it was that Rachel was going through a "premium pregnancy." To me this meant, better not breathe for the next few months. Hold your breath and keep your fingers crossed, and if you believe in God, chat with him regularly.

Actually, I do believe in God. But I was raised, like most Jews, to believe that while he is benevolent, he's also a bit of a petty egomaniac.

Max's crib arrived about a month before Rachel's due date. We'd struggled with this. Jews are not supposed to have baby showers, or order cribs, because you don't want to piss God off. He's the only one who's supposed to know what happens next, and if you act like YOU have an inkling of what's in the future—for example, if you say to a friend, "See you tomorrow, Selma!" she's likely to say, "What are you talking about? Who names anyone Selma anymore?"

Or, more likely, if she's a neurotic Jew of our generation, she's likely to say, "Kina horah!"—a term that means "Excuse me, God, no offense meant, we know YOU'RE the only one who can see into tomorrow, WE'RE nothing compared to you, you're great, you know, did we ever mention it?" That's the sum total of all Jewish prayers, by the way. There are different prayers for every holiday, and they all sound different, but when you translate them, they all boil down to, Boy, that God, is he great or what? We're nothing. We're just people. Feh. But that God—Holy Cow! Not that we think any cows are really holy, by the way, because Thou art the lord our God and we'd never even think of idolizing a craven image. Not once! Well, we put the Beatles up on a pedestal. But not as high as you, God! Congratulations on being yourself!

His name, in Yiddish, even translates as, "I am that I am." So, in other words, Jews have spent the last 4,000 years worshipping Popeye.

In our parents' generation, it was common not to just say "kina horah" when anyone said anything positive ("How are things in Glocca Mora?" "Fine, thanks, kina horah"), but to spit on the ground three times, or to make the sound of spitting, which apparently to deaf old Jewish people is "tuy tuy tuy." This is because the phrase kina horah—literally, "kin ayn horah," or "no evil eye"—is there to ward off the evil eye, whatever that is. So if the evil eye came around, of course, you spit in it. (I hope it's not God himself giving us the evil eye, because if you spit in God's eye, well, he probably wouldn't like that. Him being so terrifically great, and all.)

Anyway, so as to not piss God off, we weren't supposed to buy anything before the baby was born (kina horah). When my Uncle Artie's first kid was born, he ordered the crib, but had them leave it at the warehouse. And now that it was up to me to work my way though all this, I thought, how dumb is God to fall for a trick like that? What, God can't read the receipt tacked up on the bulletin board?

I had fended off every congratulatory phone call. I had forcibly stopped three separate groups of friends from throwing us a shower (at our age, you tend to know a lot of people, and they tend NOT to have a lot of friends having babies, so the urge to have a party was pretty unstoppable. But I stopped it). I had spit on the ground so many times the floor had become slippery and the cleaning lady fell and is suing us.

But now, I had given in to practicality (and to the idea that on the day Max was born, kina horah tuy tuy tuy, I would rather stay with him than run off to Buy Buy Baby). I had ordered The Crib.

And, now that the Evil Eye floodgates were open, The Changing Table. And the bookcase, the books, the onsies, the diapers, the wipes, the towels, the burp cloths, the swaddling blankets, the ointments, the space heater, the humidifier, the dehumidifier, the hats, the stroller, the car seat, the plastic mats, the bottles, the freezer packs, the breast pump, the thermometer, the emergency medical kit, and looked into purchasing a used car to keep in the driveway in case we had to rush the baby (kina horah) to the hospital and our car, God Forbid, shouldn't start.

We put all the stuff in his (kina horah) room.

There was no space left to put a baby.

But there we were. Supplied, educated, poised, and ready.

And still holding our breath.

I did two other things that stuck a thumb in the evil eye. One was something I allowed myself every evening, just before we went to sleep. I would crawl over and put my face right next to Rachel's enormous belly, and I would sing to the little boy waiting within.

Every night, I sang him the same song:

Yes, sir, that's my baby
No, sir, I don't mean maybe
Yes, sir, that's my baby now.

And, of course, every night, I would cry. I changed the lyrics a little ("When we meet the preacher we'll say . . ." didn't seem right. I made it "when we meet the rabbi, we'll say—careful with the knife, man!" I was trying to make Rachel laugh. But I cried, anyway, when I got to the end: Yes, sir. That's my baby now).

The other indulgence I allowed myself (kina horah, tuy tuy tuy) was to learn about the man my baby would be named after.

A few days before my Max was due, I talked to my cousin Susan. I had not talked to her since my bar mitzvah. Her dad, my father's brother, died when I was just a few years old, so I never got to know him.

His Hebrew name was Muttel Lerman, which is what his mother called him, but everyone else called him by his English name. Max.

We had decided to name our kina horah after him for two reasons. We couldn't name him after my father, Harold, because every time Rachel said the word "Harry" it came out, in her Pennsylvania accent, as "Hairy," and I couldn't spend my life with a woman calling my kid Hairy. But there was more to it than that. I already knew some of the details; Susan filled me in on the rest.

Max Lerman was born October 19, 1919, on the Lower East Side of Manhattan. He worked in burlesque, and a little in sales, but then went to work for a mobster, a Mafia guy (Susan, who is half Italian, didn't say Mafia. Italian people never say Mafia). They were bookies.

Her father, she insisted, was no street bookie, but a high-class bookie. He was a very funny man, and a very honorable one. What he said, you could count on. "I hope your son is as honorable as my dad was," she said.

His mom—and my dad's mom—was named Sadie. Grandma Sadie was not a nice woman. She was very neurotic. When my dad or Max would come visit, she would try to treat them like little kids. She would send my father to the bedroom for a nap as soon as he arrived. She would tell them they had to leave before dark and call her when they got home.

My father went along with all this babying, all his life.

Max didn't. He wouldn't take the naps, leave before dark, or follow his mother's orders on larger questions either.

Max was seeing an Italian girl named Connie. She was a dancer, Susan tells me—although I was not brave enough to ask exactly what that meant, in New York City in the 1940s. A chorus girl? A stripper? She certainly was very beautiful. Grandma Sadie hated Connie, because she was Italian. She told Max, "If you marry that girl, I'm going to jump off the roof." He told her, "Well, then you're going to jump off the roof, because I'm going to marry that girl." He did. That turned out to be Susan's mother, my Aunt Connie.

Many years later, I would visit Aunt Connie in New York, living still on the Lower East Side, in a tiny apartment on West Fourth Street. She brought out a pile of photos, two feet high, in those plasticized covers that your old class photos came in. They were all eight by ten, and had the names of all the great old New York clubs on them: The Roosevelt Grill, Monroe's Uptown House, Billy Rose's Diamond Horseshoe, the Casino de Paris. Each folder contained a glossy photo, taken from about ten feet in the air, of a long table filled with smoking, drinking, laughing postwar revelers—and at the center of each, an impossibly good-looking couple, a man with a brilliant smile and shiny wavy hair like Jimmy Cagney's, and a buxom brunette with high cheekbones and deep décolletage, one hand resting lightly on his arm. Max and Connie. The golden couple.

Max eventually became the guy who set the odds for fights, and for football games. The better he was, the more money the bookies made, and at the end of the year, the little Jew got more Christmas presents than Santa's neighbors— only Maxie's were never brightly wrapped boxes, they were just envelopes stuffed with cash. He slipped on the sidewalk one day running for a bus and went to the hospital, where it was discovered that he had advanced, inoperable cancer. Muttel "Max" Lerman, who lived a life without fear, died a few months later, on October 26, 1963, just a few weeks before President Kennedy was shot.

After all these years, Susan was so thrilled to know there would be another Max Lerman in the world. I told her that I thought her dad would be a good symbol for my son.

"My father was his own man," she said. "Men should be their own men. We should raise them to be themselves. They shouldn't live for their mothers. They should honor their mothers and fathers, but they should live for themselves, and their own wives and children. They should be their own men. I hope your son is like that."

Kina horah.

The early days of April 2002 were a nervous time in my house. George Steinbrenner was at war with the cable people in New York City. It was unclear whether we'd be able to get the Yankees on our local cable, or even on Steinbrenner's new YES Network. Needless to say, we were very, very nervous about this.

Oh, yeah. Rachel's due date was around then, too.

The first problem resolved itself simply: Yes, YES had the Yanks. Phew. That was close.

The other situation, the whole pregnancy thing, was a little more complicated.

It was a Friday morning. We were at the doctor's for a routine checkup that wound up being not so routine. Turns out, babies about to be born are supposed to have their heads firmly pressed against the center of the mother's pelvis, lined up directly in front of the exit ramp. Max had moved a little to the left. The doctor was worried, because there was the slight possibility that if labor started, the umbilical cord could come out first, followed by the baby's head, meaning he could pinch the cord between his head and Rachel's cervix, and cut off his oxygen supply.

Does everyone who has a child spend his days having horrible, terrifying conversations about things that there is just a slight possibility of, just enough of a possibility to reduce your knees to Jell-O?

The doctor had disappeared down the hall, where we saw him talking with some other people in white coats. They seemed to be huddled in great consternation, and when they saw us walking down the hall toward them, they ducked into a room.

A minute later, he emerged, and started telling us that Max was something that sounded like "blobbable," and told us that normally, they'd take a wait-and-see attitude. But since this was . . .

. . . well, since this was us, and since we were so old, and since this was our last chance . . .

. . . or did he say, because this is a premium pregnancy? . . .

. . . or was he still talking? I was sinking, falling away from the room, from Rachel, from the doctor, falling toward Max, trying to find him, to move him to the right place, to the exit ramp, I was swimming in that dark cave with the little black-and-white bald guy who kept waving at me . . . trying to hold him, to protect him . . .

. . . I'm not sure . . . I didn't feel so well . . .

The next thing I heard, though, startled me into the kind of alertness guys get when a train is headed toward their car. That adrenaline rush where you toss out the cigarette, yell at everyone to shut up, and throw the stick into gear.

They told us to head to the hospital.

I asked him if we could stop home and get Rachel's suitcase first.

He said that wasn't such a good idea.

People were waiting for us with a wheelchair for Rachel and eight thousand pages of forms for me to fill out. By the time I got to the room, Rachel was hooked up to about a dozen monitors, none of which was showing the Yankee game. They did show, however, that Max had moved himself back to the right spot on the runway, his umbilical cord trailing safely behind him in the breeze.

Phew again.

It was decided there would be no waiting for Max to come out of his comfy little apartment: We were sending in the eviction notice. A C-section was scheduled for that afternoon, but we were given one chance to shake him out with a Labor-Inducing Drug (this, in our science-soaked world, now passed for Natural Childbirth). They hooked her up to the IV and started pumping her full of the drug Pitocin, which we began calling EvictaMax.

It worked. Like crazy.

The contractions started—contractions! Just like in baby class!—and the panic attack began. Not Rachel—me. Oh, my God! I should have paid better attention! Where are my notes from baby class? When do we start the breathing thing? Is it in-out-in-out? Nurse!

Calmer people entered the room, and convinced me that we had lots of time before anything big was gonna take place. Late that afternoon I bought pizzas for the nurses and was hanging out at the nurse's station, for education purposes only, of course, since it seemed we had a lot of time to kill before the main event, when I was summoned back to Rachel's room.

Things were happening.

Rachel was in enormous pain. The baby was getting ready to come out. The anesthetist with the big needle they shove in your spine to kill the pain (ANOTHER reason men could never have babies) was busy with someone else. Rachel started trying to push Max out.

And that's when he got stubborn.

An hour of pushing went by, and then another. I tried to be helpful; I had brought a Bose CD player (they really have remarkable sound for their size; not as great as the ads would have you believe, but really, for something that small, the sound is much clearer than a normal boom box, and the bass shows very little distortion, which is really the big problem with those small speakers. Oddly, the treble was a little tinny, which you wouldn't think would be a problem at that size, but it didn't have the clarity you'd hope for. Just three years later, of course, the docking stations for the iPod would blow these Bose systems out of the water. They are absolutely stunning. Both the volume and the tone clarity seem impossible, given the size of the unit. I didn't think I needed an iPod, since I don't listen to headphones that often anymore, but man, throw your iPod and one of those docking rings in your briefcase, and you're ready to party anywhere. It's incredible. Still, for the purpose of the moment, the Bose system was more than adequate), and was alternating between some soothing massage tapes and Hepcat's right-on-the-nose "Push and Shove." I even got the nurses singing along with the chorus after awhile. Hey, it had been two hours of intense labor, somebody had to keep things light.

Which is what guys think is their reason for being in the delivery room. That, and holding your wife's hand and calling out helpful suggestions while she's pushing (like, "Push!").

This is not why you are there.

Here is why guys are in the delivery room: so when your wife throws up every five minutes in the little pan next to her head on the pillow, they don't have to waste an 18-year-old intern's valuable time to empty it.

That's why you're there.

Because, men, let's face it. In this moment, you start confronting the reality that the only order you're going to have in your life today came when you ordered the pizza for the nurses. Those months of studying the baby books, that ingrained belief that we can Fix Things (come on, dads—how many of you brought your toolbox to the hospital, just in case?)—it all flies out the window in the face of this gale force of nature all around you. There was an old *Mad* cartoon by Don Martin where the curmudgeonly Fester Bestertester—the guy with the really long feet—and his dumb-but-loveable sidekick Karbunkle found themselves stranded on the plain with a herd of buffalo charging at them. Ever wonder how they find themselves in such a predicament? Well, get a girl pregnant and wait about nine months. It feels exactly the same. (Fester Bestertester convinced Karbunkle they would be safe if they stood facing the buffalo and extended their left arms straight out. It worked about as well as a father's attempt to salvage some sense of control or order in the delivery room. Once labor starts, we are all just standing there with our left arms outstretched, the Fester Bestertesters of childbirth.)

We were now three hours into the heavy pushing. I was dying because I'd forgotten my notes from baby class. I was certain that this part was only supposed to last 20 or 30 minutes. I kept asking the nurses—hell, they ought to know, they've done this every day of their lives—and they said this was perfectly normal.

They were, not to put too fine a point on it, bullshitting us like a Vegas hooker calling you handsome.

Sometime after midnight, Max's little head started to show at the stage door. It seemed to move, just imperceptibly, every time Rachel pushed. Then, four hours after the ordeal started, it was over.

There was Max.

Soaking wet and shivering.

He was beautiful. He was perfect. He was gigantic.
He was here.

*I will tell you, Max, how I felt in the moment you arrived.
There was a frenzy of activity, but I remember the moment
with searing clarity. I had been seeing your head trying to
emerge for more than an hour. (By the way, when you finally made it out—I hope you understand, this is perfectly
normal for someone who spent as many hours squished into
the birth canal trying to be born as you did—your head
was shaped, and I say this with the utmost of love and re-
spect, like a papaya. I wasn't scared about the shape of your
head, because they had warned us of this, and I knew this
was normal, and in fact the plates of your skull slipped
back into their normal position just a few hours later.)*

*Anyway, after your head came out, the doctor managed
to get the rest of you to wriggle through. This is how I felt. I
know it sounds dumb, but my first reaction was, oh, my
God, this is an entirely different human being from me or
Rachel! This is not a mini-me, or a miniature her—it's a
separate person, not my creation, but his own person. He
doesn't even know me, never heard of the Bronx, or America's Most Wanted, or Aunt Connie—he is a stranger, one
whom we will come to know and love, but one we are just
now meeting for the first time. I know that sounds astoundingly obvious; but until now, you were not really real to
us, just an idea of a life, and it was an idea we could shape
in any way we wanted. That's what parents do before their*

child is born—they have little fantasies (like a little fantasy I had of walking to Starbucks with you on Saturday mornings—I wondered if we would ever really do that?)— fantasies that you can control, totally. No one is ever unhappy in them, no one ever disagrees, no one ever expresses another opinion. The child exists solely and totally for the amusement of the parent. But the sight of you—the actual sight of you—instantly made me realize that this is not just a reflection of my fantasies; this is a person who will grow up and have dreams and ideas and desires and fantasies of his own, and if I am a good father I will help him recognize those, and make them come true for himself—not for me, but for himself.

I hoped, in that moment, that I could remember that.

The other feeling that came over me, like a wave, was relief, mixed with equal parts exhilaration and exhaustion. I can't tell you how much fear I was trying to ignore, fear that you would never be born, that something would go wrong. It was like that fear was your twin, living in the womb with you, and when you were born, it got washed away after you, along with the placenta and the amniotic fluid, to be left behind in the hospital. I know new fears will come—they started just hours later, a whole neurotic palette of brand new fears to replace the old ones—but in that moment, the fears just washed away. I went over to the table where they were cleaning and warming you, and you were so—alive! alive! alive!—screaming and moving and fussing.

It was 1:47 in the morning. You weighed a burly eight-and-a-half pounds, you were 20 inches long, with a headful of black hair, and looked exactly like Edward G. Robinson.

Your mother wanted to hold you right away, so they brought you right over to her, and laid you on her chest. You were very quiet, we all were very quiet.

We were so happy, happy that all the pain and pushing were over, happy that you made it out so fine—healthy and heavy and perfectly formed (except for that papaya-head thing, but as I said, that cleared up right away). It was like magic—before there were just three of us, your mom, Anna, and me.

Now there were four.

4

To Dream, Perchance, of Sleep

"Everybody smile! (*click!*) Everybody smile! (*click!*) Everybody smile! (*click!*) Everybody smile! (*click!*) Everybody smile! (*click!*) Everybody smile! (*click!*) Everybody smile! (*click!*) Everybody smile! (*click!*) Everybody smile! (*click!*) Everybody smile! (*click!*) Everybody smile! (*click!*) Everybody smile! (*click!*) Everybody smile! (*click!*) Everybody smile! (*click!*)"

We are on the way home from preschool, and Max is in the backseat, with his little toy camera. Every time you push the button, a happy little woman's voice chirps, "Everybody smile!" and then there's the simulated sound of a shutter clicking. Max loves this toy, today. I ask him to stop playing with it, and he ignores me, and I contemplate reaching back and snatching it away from him, and try to decide whether inconsolable screeching and crying would be worse than this. It's a tossup.

"Everybody smile! (*click!*) Everybody smile! (*click!*) Everybody smile! (*click!*) Everybody smile! (*click!*) Everybody smile! (*click!*) Everybody smile! (*click!*) Everybody smile!

(*click!*) Everybody smile! (*click!*) Everybody smile! (*click!*) Everybody smile! (*click!*) Everybody smile! (*click!*) Everybody smile! (*click!*) Everybody smile! (*click!*) Everybody smile! (*click!*)"

This is the only time Max has stopped talking in the last few days, so there's a certain Zen peacefulness in the repetition. Usually, on the way home, our conversations veer between the incredibly specific and the wildly Dadaesque. This is how it went the day before:

"Daddy, what does my blood make after?" We have been watching something called the *Magic School Bus*, where a schoolroom full of kids led by a character voiced by Lily Tomlin gets in this bus and shrinks down and slips up one of the kids' noses, like in *Fantastic Voyage*. So we're thinking about blood a lot. "Daddy, what does my blood make after?" Max repeats.

"Max, I don't understand what you mean."

"DADDY, WHAT DOES MY BLOOD MAKE *AFTER*?" Max takes very seriously the international traveler's code—if someone who speaks a different language doesn't understand you, try talking louder.

"Max, I'm sorry, I still don't understand."

"DADDY! WHAT! DOES! MY! BLOOD! MAKE! AFTER-RRRRR!"

I decide to try a different approach.

"Um, I don't know, uh, seven?"

"Bling blong bling! That's the pinball machine!"

Somebody should make a talking doll that makes no sense, just like the kids who play with them. You could call it Salvador Dolly. I can't turn around right at the moment, but I'm sure if I looked in the backseat, there would be a big melting watch hanging from a tree.

On Rosh Hashanah, the Jewish New Year's, I was tasked by my Aunt Dottie to teach Max to say "L'shana tovah," which is Hebrew for either "Happy New Year" or "Please pass me the apple cake." Jews like to eat round things on Rosh Hashanah, so they will have a well-rounded year. Also, things with a head on them, so they will be at the head of things, not in the rear. Also, apples and honey, so we'll have a sweet year.

Are you not surprised that so many Jews wind up overweight? We imbue food with such significance. Everything you eat is symbolic. "Oh, eat these chocolate chip cookies my son, you should be a chip off the old block." "It's Simchas Torah, you must eat this banana split, we are only eating things shaped like smiles on Simchas Torah." "Tisha B'av? Eat nine pieces fried chicken! Why? Because of the destruction of the third temple in Jerusalem. What does chicken have to do with the temple? Don't ask. The rabbi explained it in his sermon this morning. You were sleeping. Just eat." "A McDonald's Happy Meal? It goes without saying! Fress, mine kinder! Eat and be happy!" Ben and Jerry's could make a mint marketing to Jews. Instead of cute hippie names like Heavenly Hash and Cherry Garcia, they could just make Your Mother Is Proud Of You Have Some Chocolate, No One Should Get Hit By A Van-Nilla, and May Your Child Get Into Harvard He's Such A Smart Boysenberry.

So, there I am, trying to teach Max to say Happy New Year. "It's Luh, sha, nah, toe, vah, Max. L'shana Tovah."

"Bowling ball bowling ball bowling ball."

"Where did you get bowling ball? It's L'shana Tovah."

"Bowling ball! Bowling ball! Bowling ball! Bowling ball! Bowling ball! Five bowling balls! They were rolling down the street and they didn't have to stop at the store for cream because it was closed and you get extra cream on Rosh Nashasa. Bowling ball! Bowling ball! Bowling ball! Bowling ball! Bowling ball!"

So, given the usual level of our discourse, I am not totally chagrined by the chant coming from the toy in the backseat. I make a mental note to throw away all AA batteries in the house, and settle in for the ride home.

"Everybody smile! (*click!*) Everybody smile! (*click!*) Everybody smile! (*click!*) Everybody smile! (*click!*) Everybody smile! (*click!*) Everybody smile! (*click!*) Everybody smile! (*click!*) Everybody smile! (*click!*) Everybody smile! (*click!*) Everybody smile! (*click!*) Everybody smile! (*click!*) Everybody smile! (*click!*) Everybody smile! (*click!*)"

We get home, and I make Max's lunch, and try to actually read the newspaper while he's eating. This is interrupted by a flying piece of macaroni and cheese, which lands in my lap.

"Max, we are not throwing macaroni and cheese, we are eating and reading newspapers. Would you like me to tell you about the Yankees? They won last night."

Max finds this funny enough to throw another piece of mac and cheese my way. The angrier I get, the funnier he finds it, and the more the macaroni flies.

So this is how my days go, now. I used to run a national television program. When people broke out of jail anywhere in the country, or shot a cop, or kidnapped a child, the call would immediately go out to someone on my staff, and they'd run into my office, and we'd put together a plan for righting whatever wrong had taken place. This was the order we imposed on the universe: We cannot stop bad things from happening, but we can control their outcome. One by one, we will rid the world of those who harm our friends and our families and, most of all, our children.

We would fly crews all over the country to get the stories; we would send people to hold the hands of the victims. There were people lined up at my office door to ask me what I wanted them to tell other people to do. And they would all do it. Quickly. These will be our rules: Just as Alex Trebek taught me, I will phrase my answers in the form of a question ("Evan, would you please get a crew to New Orleans right away?" "Chief, would you please give us all the information you have on this case, right now?" "Sedge, there's been a murder in Chicago, would you please start working on that?"), and those who respond correctly ("Certainly!" "Right away!" and "No problem!" are all acceptable) will be rewarded, and this system of positive reinforcement will create order in a sea of chaos, and each will know his task, and we will all be fast and smart and calm and good-looking.

Now, I'm bargaining: If you throw another piece of macaroni and cheese, I will take away your glowing light sticks. There. Now, if you eat four bites, you can have one light stick back.

That's how my days go now.

But I will tell you this.

My job at *America's Most Wanted*? That was hard, and because it was hard, and the results were tangible, it was satisfying. About as satisfying as a job can get.

But getting a four-year-old to stop throwing food, and sit and eat quietly?

That's a minor miracle. And because it is a minor miracle, and because the results are intangible, it is satisfying, too.

There are two reasons, I think, that dads experience this more deeply than moms, especially older dads. The going wisdom out here in parent land, of course, is that mothers are the ones who bond most deeply with their children, that after birth and breast-feeding, there's no way you can compete—what's teaching a guy to throw a curve ball, after all, compared to I Created You Whole From Inside Me And Gave You Complete Sustenance From My Own Body Both In The Year Before You Were Born And The Year After? Throw in about a year of "I want my mommy!" and guys are naturally prone to accept their supposed second-class status.

But let me tell you something.

We dads, we trudging off to work dads, we coming home tired dads, we not even there until bedtime dads, we missed the first day of school because of a business meeting in Phoenix dads, we pay the rent and fix the faucet dads, we watch the football game at home instead of at the bar with the boys dads, we cook the dinner when she's pregnant or didn't anyone notice dads, we are the patient ones. We are the silently loving ones. We are the giving ones.

The moms, well, they gave at the office, in the cosmic sense. By the time the kid is a day old, let's face it, between the nine months of pregnancy and the nightmare of childbirth, they've given about all a person has to give to gain eternal devotion. I hear my teenage stepdaughter and my five-decade-old wife yelling at each other, and I know that in that yelling there is eternal love—who else can I yell at like this, and they will always love me, because nothing can break this bond? Dads never get that. When Rachel announced she was marrying me, her then-ten-year-old daughter's first words were, "NOOOOOOOOOOOO!" followed by "NOOOOOOOOOO!"—not precisely because she didn't like me, because she did, but because she feared what would happen to that bond. And Rachel explained to her that nothing, nothing, nothing could ever happen to that bond. Because the bond between a mother and her child is stronger than the bond that holds atoms together. It is that strong. And they know that. And so they can yell at each other, and call each other names over the stupidest things—"MOM! WHERE ARE MY SHOES!" "I TOLD YOU I DIDN'T TOUCH YOUR SHOES!" "YES YOU DID! I NEED THEM NOW! FIND THEM NOW! I'M GOING TO BE LATE!" "WELL YOU WOULDN'T BE LATE IF YOU GOT UP WHEN I TOLD YOU!" "I DON'T HAVE TO GET UP EARLIER I JUST NEED YOU TO NOT LOSE MY SHOES!" "DON'T TALK TO YOUR MOTHER LIKE THAT!" "I'M NOT! WHERE ARE MY SHOES?!" "YES YOU ARE! DID YOU LOOK IN YOUR ROOM?!" "OF COURSE, HOW COULD YOU EVEN ASK A QUESTION LIKE THAT?!" "HERE ARE THE GREEN SHOES. WHY CAN'T YOU WEAR THE GREEN SHOES?!" "BECAUSE!" "BUT IF YOU DON'T GO NOW YOU'RE GOING TO BE LATE!" "THEN FIND MY SHOES!" "DON'T TALK TO YOUR MOTHER LIKE THAT!"—and a minute later, the erstwhile shoes are located (in her room, of course; turns out she had taken her desire not to walk up the stairs as proof that they couldn't be up there), and the storm has passed, and they are talking in hushed tones at the front door—"Did you take your cough medicine?" "Yes, Mommy." "OK, if you feel sick later, you go right to the nurse." "OK, Mommy, I love you." "I love you. Go. The carpool is out front." "Can we go to Georgetown after school and buy me some new shoes?" "We'll see." "Please?" "We'll see. If you don't have too much homework." "Pleeeeease?" "We'll see what time it is when it's time to go." "Pretty please?" "OK. As long as you finish your homework." "Thank you Mommy, I love you." "I love you too. Now go."

Dads don't get that.

They don't have that atom thing.

And so, from the time the baby is conceived, dads swim upstream, trying to push against the tide and achieve some measure of that closeness, that unbreakable devotion, that unswerving loyalty. They sing and cuddle and change diapers and read stories and make funny faces and tell jokes and do a thousand other things to try to break the code that links the child to its mother, to try to replicate it in the daddy laboratory. Moms don't have to work that hard. Dads do—they are the Avis of parenting, always trying harder. But no matter how hard they work, they will never replicate the atom thing. Dads don't understand, for example, how it's possible that the mom and the child don't love each other *despite* the yelling and screaming—but *because* of it. Because it is proof, for both of them, the mother and the child, that the bond is unbreakable. It's like the luggage in the commercial. Someone says the luggage is unbreakable? You give it to the gorilla, of course. Let him toss it around, jump up and down on it, that sort of thing. To prove to yourself that it is unbreakable. That's what the mother and child are doing—proving to themselves that they have the Samsonite of relationships.

Dads are more like an L.L. Bean backpack. Pretty damn durable, in its own way, but you wouldn't want to give it to the gorilla.

Groucho Marx famously noted that there are hundreds upon hundreds of songs about mothers; he tossed off "Mammy" and "Mom They're Making Eyes at Me," but of course he could have added "Mother Macree" and "My Yiddeshe Momma" and that "M is for the many things she gave me" ditty, or "Mother" (Lennon's or Chicago's), "Mother and Child Reunion," "Mother Earth," "My Mother's Eyes," even "Mother's Little Helper." And what songs, he asked, have there been written about fathers? Two—"Pop Goes the Weasel," and "Oh What a Crumb Was My Old Man."

(To right this wrong, Groucho performed the following, quite telling, number, penned by Harry Ruby:

Today, father, is Father's Day,
And we're giving you—a tie.
It's not much we know, it is just our way of showing you,
We think you're a regular guy!
You say that it was nice of us to bother,
But it really was a pleasure to fuss,
For according to our mother, you're our father,
And that's good enough for us,
Yes that's good enough for us.)

Even Mary, mother of Jesus, has a thousand songs. She's all you hear about, all Christmas season. Mary this, Mary that, the child the son of Mary, blah blah blah. How many songs did Joseph get? I think when the Yankees play "Cotton-Eyed Joe" during the seventh-inning stretch, that's supposed to be about him, but that's really it, basically. And why is the most urban and urbane team in all of sports playing "Cotton-Eyed Joe" during the seventh-inning stretch, anyway? Where, in the great pantheon of New York songs, did that show up? With all of Broadway and Tin Pan Alley and Harlem to choose from, how did we get a bluegrass foot-stomper? Somebody call Steinbrenner.

Because they have so much ground to make up, dads try so much harder, are so much kinder and softer. Why does everybody think it's the other way around?

Simple.

It's Oprah's fault.

Oprah, and Sally Jessy, and a few others of their ilk, have perpetuated the fifties myth of the distant cold Dad In The Gray Flannel Suit. It simply doesn't reflect reality, anymore; for one thing, the materials you can get now are so much more slimming. But also, 50 percent of women in this country work outside the home, and about 10 percent of the men are bums like me who don't. So a majority of this country is not divided into men who work and women who stay home. Those families exist, but they're a minority. A loud, vocal minority, but a minority nonetheless, like compassionate conservatives.

It's the non-working women, however, who are not only watching the daytime talkies, but attending them sitting in the audiences. And what happens when one of the guests comes on to hawk her latest book, *Stone Walls And Ice: The Story Of Fathers In America*, or the recently popular *"Dad:*

What The Hell Is Wrong With Him Anyway?"—do these women stand up in the audience and shout, "Fraud! My father always slipped me ten extra bucks when I went out on a date! He wanted me to have cab fare home and didn't ask for it back when I got a ride! I never told him I was buying pot with it, even though he probably knew, but he never made a big deal of it! What a great fucking guy!"

I think not.

This is where dads could use the same PR agents that the three-year-olds got. Because when we talk about Real Men, we're not talking just about NASCAR, beer, and that woman with the humongous breasts from the GoDaddy ads that keep getting bounced off the Super Bowl (the ads, not the breasts). I'm talking about the rest of us—dutifully taking our Lipitor and eating that shitty fiber cereal to keep our cholesterol down, dutifully showing up at parent-teacher night to sit in the tiny chairs with our knees sticking up to our noses so we can hear about how we can help our children develop fine motor skills by hiding pennies in the Play-Doh, dutifully working year after year for people who are not smarter than we are so that we can afford those moments on the weekend where we take the kids to the toy store and don't have to steer them away from the aisle with the big remote control trucks. We just try harder. Does that actually make us better parents than mothers? I don't know. But I do know that we try harder, and it's that reality (along with our unswerving, unshakable, and totally mistaken faith in our ability to reason with our children) that makes us who we are. This is what we need to get out a press release on. Sedge, would you please start working on that?

Actually, there's one other reason that a father's love is, in its own way, deeper and more complex than a mother's. Especially older fathers.

It's that men are more fixated on death.

All the great existentialist philosophers were men: Sartre, Camus, and, um, well, there you go, they were both men. We all read them in college, men and women; but whereas women got an A on the tests and moved on, men . . . hesitated.

Thinking, you know, there is that question.

What if this is all there is?

I don't know any women who continue to fret over this, year in and year out, once they've tossed their mortarboards in the air.

But when a man turns the curve at fifty, and can see that stretch to the horizon in front of him . . .

Things stop making sense.

You start to wonder, quietly, whether it matters if the Yankees win their 27th championship, because if there is no heaven, then you will cease to exist and therefore cease to care, because someday they will reach their 100th championship, long after you are gone, and who cares whether that happens 300 or 301 years from now, since you're not going to be watching it, and even the people who do get to see it will die and be forgotten as well. I felt very sad that my own father died before Max was born, and never got to meet him, but there's a tiny part of me, one I don't like to look at and don't like to talk about, that says, well, what if there is no heaven and he's just . . . you know, dead . . . well, what would it matter if he ever met Max, since he certainly won't know it now, and Max won't remember it anyway? You start to see everything around you, and know it will die, and you are overwhelmed by a sense of futility, of hopelessness. Why should I read another sentence of this book, why should I get up from this chair, or continue to sit in it, since I will die and forget that I did or did not read, did or did not get up? How does one go on, when nothing matters?

And as you think this, a four-year-old child runs in the room with a balloon. "Look what I found!" he yells. "It's orange! It's my favorite!" And he hits you with the balloon, and laughs hysterically, and hits you again, and laughs hysterically again, and you realize, I am in the presence of someone who has conquered time, because for him all of time is compressed into this perfect moment, this blissful moment, this moment that will never end. Because this orange balloon matters, matters enormously, and if this orange balloon matters, then everything matters.

Everything matters.

It is, ultimately, the lesson that the child teaches the father. Because, at our age, we start to forget that. Moms don't forget it, but dads do.

And so we need to be taught, over and over.

Which is what our children do. They teach us this one lesson, over and over.

Everything matters.

It is the lesson Max has been teaching me since our first days together.

We brought him home from the hospital on the third day of his life. It's very scary to bring the baby home. Suddenly, there are no nurses around in case . . . well, you know, dads spend 95 percent of their brain cells, for the rest of their lives, finishing that sentence. In case he stops breathing, starts choking, turns blue, in case he won't eat, won't sleep, in case I drop him, step on him, spill hot coffee on him, in case he develops boils or polka dots or stripes, in case he gets wedged in between the dishwasher and the cabinet, in case his ears fall off, in case he grows antennas. You've spent months learning everything that could possibly go wrong, two days having somebody else check to make sure nothing's going wrong—how are his bilirubins? Are we supposed to be checking his bilirubins? Rachel, did you ask how to check the bilirubins? What the hell are bilirubins, anyway? I feel so sorry for the first kid who had whatever disease that is, where the level of something drops precipitously low, and they don't have a name for it yet, so they say what the hell, just name it after the kid. And the rest of his life it's, "Hi, I'm Billy Rubin," and people are like, "How cruel of your parents to name you after the disease," and you're like, "No, that's me." It's like, "Hi, my name is Advanced Gonorrhea."

And what if Rachel and I simultaneously have a fainting spell? I've never actually fainted in my life, but now, it was all I could imagine—I saw myself like the guys in the cartoons, little X's on my eyes, a little spiral coming out of the top of my head, exclamation points emitting from my temples. What if I faint? Who is going to take care of the baby?

I think as you get older you worry about this much more. My friend David just interviewed the great underground cartoonist Harvey Pekar ("Don't call me a curmudgeon," he said when David walked in. "Everybody calls me a curmudgeon"). Pekar worries about everything. He locks his keys in the car all the time, and worries about people breaking in and stealing the car. He has a great phrase for this: "I catastrophize everything," he told David. That's what being a parent is about. You catastrophize everything.

Life is different anyway, when you reach the age where there's just the outside possibility that any second you could be grabbing your chest and saying "Rosebud." I'll tell you, all of a sudden you understand why old guys complain about how slow a baseball game is. "Come on! Pitch the damn ball already! I want to see the ninth inning before I die altogether!" We thought we were so wild as teenagers, that we took such chances. Oh yeah? Go a few months without checking your cholesterol. That's living on the edge.

So how could you make that fear any worse? Easy. Let the guy hold a baby, leave him alone in the house, and let the phrase enter his head "I hope I don't have a heart attack before my wife comes home." You don't need to feel your wrist to take your blood pressure after that—you can actually see the veins popping out of your neck in three-quarter time.

But oddly, at the same time, a strange peace came over me, as well. The first time I was alone in a room with Max and he started crying, I decided he looked . . . cute. Just so cute, that tiny cry, that wide-open mouth, those pristine gums. It calmed me down. I knew that if I stayed calm it would help keep the baby calm too, so I left it as a little posthypnotic suggestion for myself—when he cries, let it calm me down. And it started to work. Which is good, because that first day home, he did a hell of a lot of calming.

When he wasn't crying to calm me down, or crying for a million other reasons I could imagine (Rachel! I think his skin is too tight! We should take him back to the hospital to check!), I walked him around the house, introducing him to his new world. For months afterward, whenever he was upset, I could calm him down by taking a tour of the lamps, all of whom, of course, were named Mister Lamp. There was only one song I wanted to hear, and I played it over and over until Rachel threw the CD out into the backyard. It was Dylan, singing "New Morning":

Can't you feel that sun a-shinin'?
Ground hog runnin' by the country stream
This must be the day that all of my dreams come true
So happy just to be alive
Underneath this sky of blue
On this new morning, new morning
On this new morning with you.

By the time we brought Max home, I had already become one of those doting parents who not only hovers on everything the baby does ("Look, Rachel, a tarry stool! Just like they said! That's a good sign! And it's his second one today! He's a genius!"), but thinks the rest of the world hovers on everything the child does too—and uses the Internet to fulfill that imagined fascination ("Picture 47 is Max sleeping in the kitchen. Picture 48 is Max sleeping in the living room. If you look carefully at Picture 49, you can see where he spit up on his sleeve"). But in my defense, I will say that those first days were pretty fascinating.

The doctors were a little concerned when we told them that Max was eating only once a day—but they were reassured when we explained that that one feeding went on for 23 hours. On the feeding front, Rachel remained in charge of incoming—Max and Rachel bonded on that concept just fine, thank goodness—and I was in charge of outgoing. And let me tell you, Max was one outgoing child. I began wondering if Hefty made a lawn-and-leaf-sized bag that converted into a diaper. How could such a tiny being—those impossibly tiny, crinkly fingers, those little jet-black eyes the size of peas, those chunky little chicken-thighs, that no-longer-papaya-shaped head—how could such a tiny being produce such an inordinate volume of poop?

Rachel did not change a diaper for the first two weeks of Max's life. I changed them all, I did all the cooking, the cleaning, I got Anna up and fed her and made sure she took her Dexedrine before carpool. This is what dads do.

And this is what older dads do: They go out to get the papers, which they will never ever have time to read, and they fall asleep on the front lawn. All across America, if you drive the suburban roads at 7:30 in the morning, you will see teenagers running off to carpools, and fathers snoring in the crabgrass. Never for very long; but I would get down on one knee to pick up the paper—my back no longer bending so much as, well, not-bending—and, from there, the lawn would just look so inviting, and standing up seeming like such an arduous task. And somehow, I would find myself with grass up my nose a minute later.

And then I would go back and resume my duties.

Weeks went by, slowly, like, this, and, it, all, seemed . . . like . . . one . . .

long . . .

slow . . .

day.

Because when you don't sleep, that's what life becomes. One long, slow day. On good nights, Max would breast-feed about midnight. Around three, he would wake up and say, "You know, I could do with a snack—and while I'm up, would you mind changing this diaper? It's a bit—well, messy, you know." So we feed him and change him, and he's exhausted. "Guys, this is too much! You and your middle-of-the-night parties. I'm gonna go crash in the bassinet. See you in the morning"—which came, of course, about three hours later. Still, this passed as miraculously easy in daddy worlds. Two three-hour naps? Consider yourself blessed.

It didn't last.

Soon, the little snacks became hour-long cryfests, unless you walked the floor with him. Soon, the three-hour naps in the night became—well, no one can remember, because you are too tired.

In the daytime, he'd fall out now and then, and everyone told us to sleep when the baby sleeps, which is a bit didactic ("Rachel! Put down the paper! Quick! His eyes are closed! Get the hell into bed now! We should be sleeping!"), but we figured we should store up while we could. Once you're at the age when "Stay up and watch Letterman" is considered a major event, you're really too old for this.

There is only one thing that gets you through.

The baby smell.

You wake up for the ninth time, and it's your turn to quiet the baby, so you take him in your arms, and walk the floors, singing, as I said earlier, the canon of baby songs (that first week, "Be My Baby" and "Yes Sir That's My Baby" were in the high rotation, along with "Baby It's You" and, of course, the song everybody only knows the chorus to, but can sing it for an hour to a crying baby—Smokey Robinson's "Ooo Baby Baby")—as you walk, and rock, and shush, and cuddle, you dip your cheek to his downy little head, and that baby smell wafts up, and you drink it in deep, and all is suddenly right with the world, and you are ready for another hundred choruses of "Is You Is Or Is You Ain't My Baby." Because, in that moment, that smell has linked you forever. And yes, you is my baby. You certainly is.

I found that I could just . . . STARE at him, for an hour. Just to see, to feel the wonderment, even in his sleep: how could a hand be so tiny? How did he know to grow exactly one fingernail for each finger? When he twitches like that in his sleep, what is he thinking? And when he was awake, he would . . . LOOK at me. He would look at me! He would look away, and then . . . LOOK BACK! Anna hated this. She would say, "Ooh, weird! He's staring at me! Make him stop!"—But I couldn't get enough of it.

I kept thinking of the time we got those sea monkeys in the mail from the back of the comic book, and in the ads you saw lots of little monkeys running around your house, wearing funny hats and swinging baseball bats, but when you ordered them and they finally came and you put the little orange capsule in the water, and woke up the next day, you found out they were really just called "sea monkeys" but were actually brine shrimp, funny little fish that look like prehistoric cockroaches. But what if they were really monkeys? Real, actual monkeys? Wouldn't that have been cool?

Now, finally, here was my own, little monkey boy. Gigantic, compared to a brine shrimp, too.

I was quite tired.

And I was quite at peace.

Eventually, I had to go back to work, and Rachel let me out of one or two of the nighttime feeding-and-changing details, but still the lack of sleep and the separation from my little monkey boy wore heavily on me.

Around the office, there were three other guys who had new babies. These were guys with resources I didn't have (like hair on top of their heads, for one thing, and the youthful ability to stay up all night, for another). The Travails Of The Night are, of course, the only things that people with newborns talk about: Guys with babies come up to us on the street and whisper, "So, how much are you getting?"—and, while we've heard the question before in other venues, we know immediately they're talking about sleep. So we share the information: Max is sleeping three hours at a stretch (ergo, so is Rachel). Phil is sleeping six on work nights (and assuaging his guilt, in the Jewish tradition, by cooking and cleaning). Anna is staying up later than all of us. One night we met a lady who was getting nine. We hate her.

We actually got out of the house without Max a few times, that first month. The first time, we went to the White House Correspondents Dinner, and were introduced to Colin Powell. I told him that this was Rachel's first time away from the baby. "How old?" he asked. "Three weeks," said Rachel. Powell, without another word, reached into his pocket, pulled out a cell phone, and said, "Here, call home, you'll feel better." (Later, when I called Anna with this news, she screamed, "You mean you're calling me on *Colin Powell's cell phone?*" When I told her I wasn't, that I was using my own cell phone, she was crestfallen, for I had proved once again that parents are the uncoolest people on the planet.)

If it is true, as Rachel tells me, that much of our behavior is genetically rooted in our hunter-gatherer ancestry, then it made perfect sense that Rachel, as Gatherer-Woman, began handling many of the varied tasks involved in newlybabying (I learned, from reading all the books around our house on "parenting," that people in the baby field are allowed to make up any verbs they want), but while she covered the waterfront, I, as Hunter-Man, became obsessed with only one task.

Stalking the smile.

It was true: Max had started smiling. It was as wonderful as everyone told us it would be, as wonderful as listening to Van Morrison sing "I'm heaven when you smile," dragging out "heaven" to four syllables; it was just about as wonderful a feeling as there is—when he smiled at *you*, of course. Mostly, he smiled at (in order) his mother, his sister, the lamp, his raccoon, air, the television, his blanket, the box of wipes on the changing table, me, and me with a camera.

This made proving the Existence Of The Smile somewhat akin to proving the Existence Of God: It became the motivating factor in our lives, but you had to take it on faith.

Mothers don't seem to get obsessed with the camera thing. But dads—we have to get it on tape. Or on film. The advent of digital technology only worsened this obsession. Now, we not only spent hours bothering everyone in the house for one more shot, but several more hours trying to figure out how to upload (or download) the pictures to our computers, inload (or outload) them to a folder, rightload (or leftload) them to the printer, and dropload them onto actual paper. Then, of course, there was the nightlong process of trying to e-mail them to relatives, and, if one actually accomplished that, the long phone calls the next morning in which you try to explain to various aunts and uncles how to open the pictures on their computers ("No, Aunt Dottie. The keyboard is the thing with the letters on it. The mouse is the other thing with the wire coming out of it. What? No, that would be the toaster. You can't get the pictures there. Yes, I know we gave you that toaster. Yes, I'm glad you like it. Listen, instead of trying to open the picture, can you just come visit the kid and see him for yourself?").

Actually, I didn't go fully digital when Max was born. Luddite that I am, I stayed with film. This meant shooting roll after roll, running them to the drugstore, waiting until the next day, and finding out I had 147 pictures of my thumb.

Double prints, no less.

And as this endless delirious day unfolds, we realize that these are truly the times that try men's souls—for as we go through the transformation that comes with having a baby, we are faced with nothing short of a revolution in our lives; each of the little victories and defeats, the sleep and the poop and the feedings and the not-feedings and the cameras and the smiles and the tears and the thousands of tiny tasks that now make up our lives—this is what our revolution is made of. Tiny victories, tiny defeats, all little battles in the big war against despair; fighting to keep it all together one more day, trying to bring order against the rising tide of chaos, and knowing that, for all intents and purposes, we're actually up shit creek without a paddle.

The next little battle coming over the horizon is figuring out how to talk to the baby. There are two schools of thought on this. When we started out, mine, shared by my extremely cool teenage stepdaughter, which makes it obviously correct, was: Talk to the baby in normal English. Do not make cooing sounds; remember there is no such word as "oogly-moogly"; and, in general, stay with simple declarative sentences. The books we had around the house (and when I say "books" I mean it in the sense of "somebody purchased the Library of Congress and dumped it in your living room")—the books we had around the house supported me in this theory, saying that babies who spend more time around fathers talk sooner because of the father's tendency to use regular language from an earlier age, which stimulates the language center of the brain.

That's one theory.

The other, favored by most women, is: Speak to them like they are idiots.

"Ooh, is zat da mooby dooby baby? Is zat a mooby dooby? Is zat what it is? Is zat a mooby dooby?" If I were Max, I'd be thinking, for Chrissakes, how the hell do I know if I'm a mooby dooby baby. You're the grownup, you figure it out. I have diapers to pee in.

But something snaps in the daddy's brain when he sees how the baby reacts. Our friend Ellen would put her face really close to Max's, smile at him with a smile so wide I thought her lips would meet in the back and the top of her head would fall off, nod her head up and down vigorously and shout, "Bla bla bla! Ha ha ha!" (Yes, that is a direct quote)—and Max loved it. He was so happy to see Ellen. His face would light up when she walked in the room: Oh, here comes that standup comic! The one who does the bla-bla bit! That kills me! Hey, lady! Come over here! Lay that bla bla on me! I be needing some bla bla right about now!

This works at a father's psyche.

Until he snaps.

And he, too, becomes an idiot.

Maybe it was jealousy. Or maybe babies release chemicals that stimulate the goofiness centers of the parental brain. For whatever reason, one day I just looked Max straight in the eye and uttered the time-honored phrase, "ugga-bugga BOOP!"—which Max, of course, found to be the funniest joke he'd ever heard. I mean, it ranked right up there with the Bla Bla Lady routine. So, of course, I now found myself walking around the house with him, repeating my killer joke—"ugga-bugga BOOP!"—which never failed to get a laugh.

For a while.

The joke, apparently, wore thin; but, like all parents who taste the joys of successful infant stand-up comedy, I started seeking new material, walking around the house blathering like an idiot ("labba da babba—yap yap!"), reinforced by the occasional smile. I was forced to undergo this process in secret, since Anna was still keen on the "real language" idea—and when she caught me in full "goo-bop-a-loogie" mode, she would sneak up behind me and yell, "English, Philly, English!"

But I would not be dissuaded.

There is another strange language change that comes over parents. In an effort to keep talking to the baby, so as to keep him calm—but while you're still trying to get something done—you run out of stuff to say. So you start narrating your day, in a series of rhetorical questions and redundant affirmative responses.

"Is Daddy making toast? Yes! Yes! Daddy's making toast! Yes, he is! Is this toast? Yes, this is toast!"

It's a wonder they let the kids anywhere near us.

This is also, by the way, how the blues were born—they were an effort to stretch these minor observations out into longer dissertations, with a beat you could rock the baby to. I have actually caught myself singing this:

*"Oh Daddy's making toast, he's making toast all day
   long. . . .
Daddy's making toast, he's making toast all day long . . .
I hope that he don't burn it, 'cause that would be
   extremely wrong."*

There are, I am embarrassed to say, many, many more verses to this song, but I will spare you.

Max, for his part, began developing much more normally than his dad. He would be alert for hours at a time, watching the world around him: He especially loved watching his Baby Mozart video. This is part of a series known as the Baby Einstein tapes, which are simply videotapes of various children's toys, either in action or rolling across the screen, shown to classical music. They must have cost about seven bucks to film, and to date have netted—I looked it up—9.3

bazillion dollars. Every baby loves them, and every parent can't stand them, because they're too busy thinking: Why the hell didn't I come up with this?

Max also, at the age of three months, picked up his sister's love of infomercials (his favorite: Jennifer Lopez for Madre Restaurant).

And, startlingly, at the age of three months, he started speaking. His main point seemed to be "Oooooh-WA! WOH!" which he repeated, emphatically, and then stared at you quizzically, because you just didn't seem to be getting the point.

There are all sort of little growth milestones that pop up around three months. Here's one strange one: we took him to the doctor to get checked, and they measured him and he was literally, off the charts. He was in the 100th-plus percentile for his age, which I interpret to mean that he is taller than every baby that ever existed including himself, but they reassured us that there are lots of babies in the 100th-plus percentile, confirming my belief that people become doctors because they can't do math.

Anna had just returned from Japanese camp on Max's three-month birthday. She greeted Max with, "*Konnichiwa!*" to which Max responded, "Oooh-WA! WOH!" and I replied, "Ugga-bugga-BOOP!"

And they say families don't talk anymore.

That first summer, we traveled with Max a lot. At three months, they're pretty simple to travel with. My sister-in-law calls them Luggage That Eats.

Among our stops: Anna was enrolled in something called Camp Broadway, where she was going to learn to sing even louder than she already did, and so we headed to New York City for a week.

Max decided, around then, that he had slept quite enough in his short life, thank you very much, and now, at night he had much better things to do.

Babies, around that age, develop an interior altimeter. They cry, you pick them up, they stop crying. You hold them until they fall asleep, which usually takes no more than five or six hours. You start to lower them back into their bassinet and . . . howling! Incredible shrieks! My goodness, I'm almost at sea level, man! Up, up I say! Ah, there, 3.5 feet above the floor, much better. I'll stop screeching now. Thanks. Don't try that again, bub.

And so you stand there, bleary and hallucinatory from lack of sleep, rocking back and forth, wondering if you can sleep standing up like a horse, mumbling reassuring words to your little bundle of joy, watching the sun come up again on another goddamn fucking when can I get some fucking sleep around here fucking glorious day.

But finally, the baby falls asleep, and you put him gently in his bassinet, and he does not wake up, and you catch at least a three-minute nap, and awake refreshed, forgetting your fury of the hour before, knowing only the peace that comes from this joyful, blessed, tiny figure in your life, now crying his tiny change-my-diaper-please cry, and you smile, forgetting how tired you are, and cradle him in your arms and bring him to the makeshift changing table you've created in the hotel room out of the antique desk and sixteen bath towels, and you lay him ever-so-softly down on the table, and remove his tiny diaper, and take a moment to revel in the miracle of that perfect, soft tushie, those chubby little legs, that trusting, trusting, trusting smile.

Until, of course, he pisses in your eye.

And so another day of our vacation begins.

There are so many things that no one told you before you had a baby—deep, spiritual truths that you only learn from spending time in the presence of your little miracle.

For example: Babies, it turns out, are great chick magnets.

In the mornings, I would take Max for a stroll toward Central Park (with the way he was sleeping, we both needed a cup of coffee), and the kind of astoundingly beautiful if slightly undernourished women you see only in New York would walk up and screech, "Oh, so adorable!"

"Thanks!" I would say; then, with disappointment, "Oh, you mean the baby."

This would not garner the slightest response, because the supermodels were busy making the biggest-eyed, widest-mouthed goofy faces at Max, who would oblige them with his killer toothless smile, which would make them coo even louder.

So, ironically, I found myself surrounded by the kind of women who wouldn't have given me the time of day when I actually had any reason to care. There was, of course, only one solution.

We started renting Max out to single men for $20 an hour. For an extra five bucks, we gave them a plausible explanation of what they were doing with a baby.

Other than that, traveling with Max was, for the most part, a breeze. For the first time since I was fourteen years old, I took off three weeks in a row, to spend some time getting to know my son. After our week in the city, we headed for

Rachel's family's lake house in upstate New York, a retreat for the mind and soul, the place where we had first learned Rachel was pregnant, and a place so small that we were assured of all getting on each other's nerves as quickly as possible.

In the afternoons, Anna would be off with her friends, and so Max and I would send Rachel away, and go out on the porch, and sit on the rocker, and just get to know each other.

Here's what I got to know first:

Babies have very short attention spans.

Max was a wonderful audience, and loved it when I would play with him, or sing to him (dads are a little like Doctor Frankenstein: "Oh, so no one wants to hear me sing, eh? Well, I'll CREATE A LIFE that will LOVE my singing! Ha ha ha!").

And, I must admit, there were times during the day when he would sit blissfully for an hour, chewing on a fist, contemplating the complexity of the universe as embodied in the color of your T-shirt. In fact, much of the day, he was just a happy guy, watching with fascination and amusement as the world paraded by.

But then Doctor Jekyll turned into Mister Max, and he began to get bored, and he would scream bloody murder, until you found something to distract him, which lasted on average about twenty seconds.

So there we are, out on the porch, struggling to stave off hysteria. Typical interaction:

Me: "Look Max! It's Mister Bumblebee! Here he comes!"

Max: "Ha ha ha! I love Mister Bumblebee!" (Actually, what he said was "blaaaaaaa!"—but I will interpret for you.)

Me: "Here he is! It's Mister Bumblebee!"

Max: "Blaaaa!" (Translation: "HAHAHAHAHA! Mister Bumblebee is so funny!")

Me: "Yes, it's Mister Bumblebee, all right!"

Max: "WAAAAA!" ("I HATE Mister Bumblebee! Get him away!
Why do you torture me like this?")

Me: "Ok, ok, here's, um, Mister Worm! Look, it's Mister
Worm!"

Max: "Blaaaa!!" ("Ha ha ha! I love Mister Worm. . . .")

After a half an hour, we have played with every toy twice,
and I have sung every song I ever heard; we have played
"clap clap clap hello" (a big favorite) so often that my palms
are chapped—and Max is getting to be like a restless Cat-
skills crowd, chomping on his pacifier like a nickel cigar and
calling out, "Yeah, yeah, what else you got, buddy?"

He is, of course, doing his part of the entertainment as
well, which consists mainly of exhibiting how many different fluids he can produce from various orifices (if we could
only make a car that ran on baby drool, we could end our
dependence on foreign oil, and achieve world peace). He
is also practicing his latest trick, which is placing his foot
into his mouth (Rachel: "So like his dad!").

But we manage to work our way through it all until
Rachel comes home for feeding time (which, by the way,
takes a lot of ego strength for a dad. You look at your baby
at your wife's breast, and you're supposed to be in awe of
the miracle before you, but you can only think: You know,
I'm definitely not the most important person in EITHER of
their lives right now).

When you travel with a baby, people require you to
fulfill the fantasy that every moment with a baby is pure

bliss, and that your life is being lived on a higher plane of consciousness.

It does seem that way sometimes, but it turns out just to be the delirium caused by the sleep deprivation.

Max continued his pattern of sleeping for no more than two hours at a time. Most guys like it when their wives look good, but give a man a few months of sleeplessness, and he looks at his wife one day, and she looks beautiful, and has retained her sense of humor, and you begin thinking: Is she cheating on me? Is she sleeping around behind my back? (Not sex, mind you—literally, sleeping?) Is she sneaking off for a quickie nap when I'm not looking? What the hell is going on here?

In fairness to Max, however, I should note that his cries in the night became fairly short-lived, and were quickly quieted with a hug or a snack from the Big Boob Café (or, as Rachel says: "Maybe I'll just top him off").

These were, of course, unlike his cries when Rachel was away. If she'd grab a few sane moments by going out with some friends at night, and I was staying with him, Max wailed uncontrollably: "What is the MATTER with you people!? Don't you realize that Mom is gone? The world as we know it has ended! Chaos rules in a void of darkness! All is lost! Oh, woe!"

This goes on for about a half hour, with Max only driven to deeper despair by my feeble attempts to console him, those attempts offering clear proof that I do not understand the utter futility of the situation—until, in an utterly random moment born of my desperation, we have this conversation:

Me: "Look Max! It's Mister Bumblebee! Here he comes!"
Max: "Ha ha ha! I love Mister Bumblebee!"

And so it goes.

Bliss?

Well, there is that moment, when he is at his mom's breast, and stops feeding for a second, and looks up at her with that astounding, toothless grin, as if to say, oh, I get it. I see what's going on here. Hey, thanks!

Or the glee, the unmitigated, full-body-shaking, high-pitched-giggling glee, when he hears you launch into "Do Wah Diddy."

Or that moment when he is crying at night, and you pick him up, and his little hand grabs a fistful of chest hair, and he nuzzles his nose against your arm, and he falls back asleep, and the hand relaxes, and you're about to put him back in his bassinet, but you don't—you just sit in the rocker, patting his bottom, contemplating the simplicity of the universe, as embodied in his tiny, tiny snore.

There is that.

April 13, 2003. Your first birthday. Can it possibly be? I can barely remember what life was before you. It certainly wasn't this. . . . Engaging. Meaningful. Tiring. Important. Fascinating. Tiring. Relentless. Blissful. Heart-rending. Joyous. Tiring. Lovely.

Last week, I took you to New York to see the Statue of Liberty, because I think on their first birthday everybody should go look at a statue of a woman holding up one candle.

But today is your real first birthday, and today we had your party. You didn't really get what was going on, but you loved playing with your balloons, and you loved the toy train that Aunt Eleanor and Aunt Robin gave you, and you really, really loved . . . Cake! Your first sugar. Something tells me it won't be your last.

So, anyway, at the end of the night—even though we knew we should be getting to sleep—your mom and I sat down and watched all our home movies of you. A Year of Max. We couldn't believe it—how much you've changed, how fascinated we were at each milestone, and yet how hard it is to remember those milestones now (was it really so fascinating that you sat up? That you reached for a toy? That you could crawl backwards down the stairs? This all seems so far away now, writing this on your first birthday, as it must seem to you, now, reading it whenever you might be reading it). Your first crawl, your first bath, your first food, all these moments that went by in the blink of an eye. Every adult has said this to every child, and every child has looked at them as though they were speaking Martian, but I will say it to you anyway: Now, when you are young, time seems to go very slowly. You will not be able to believe how far away the party you're waiting to go to is, how far away the summer is, how far away your next birthday is. You can't believe the millions of tons of time you have ahead of you to plow through. And we know that this will not last, that soon, sooner than you think, you will say, time is slipping away so fast! And you will do things to try to drag your foot, to slow things down. Like videotaping events, and writing notes like these in your son's journal, ways to try to store time in a bottle, save it forever, save all these precious moments from fading away so fast, so fast, so fast.

I love you, my son, more than I have ever loved before. Happy birthday.

5

There Goes My Baby

By the time Max was a year old, we had to face the fact: We were terrible, terrible parents, weak of spirit, spoiling our baby hopelessly, forever. I knew this because many, many people told me this, when I admitted to them what I admit to you now.

Namely, that we let Max sleep in bed with us.

We didn't mean to. It was just this: Max was a wonderful boy, and he still liked to wake up every two hours at night to tell us how wonderful he is. We had moved him, by now, from the bassinet next to our bed into a crib in his own room. This, of course, meant only one thing to me: Yay! Sex is back!

Yes, my friends, I was still that naïve. Our moments alone, and awake, in bed, were to be quite few and far between.

When Max cried, I would go to his crib (or, to be accurate, more often, Rachel would go to his crib, and I would sympathize. But sometimes, it was me. Really.). I lifted him up, and he would be asleep again, almost as soon as he was in my arms.

And he would be screaming again, as soon as I would try to lower him into the crib. The altimeter he had experimented with was now a finely tuned instrument, going off like a fire alarm if you even started to lower him into his crib.

After about twenty minutes of this, at three in the morning, I come to the brilliant conclusion: You know what, Max? You wanna sleep, I wanna sleep. Let's do it your way.

So I cradle him in my arms, and bring him to bed, and, for safety, carefully move all the pillows and blankets away, and shush Rachel when she yells, "Hey, where are all the pillows and blankets!?"—and he nuzzles himself under my arm, and we all drift off, blissfully, to sleep, Mommy, Daddy, baby, cuddled together.

This, of course, was, according to friends, relatives, acquaintances, nosy taxi drivers, and perfect strangers, the absolute worst thing we could do.

True story: At a bat mitzvah, I admitted this sin to a friend of my Aunt Dottie's. Her exact response: "You are spoiling that child! He will never sleep in his own bed! This is a terrible mistake! You must stop that, right now!"

Then, more quietly: "I hope you don't take this as criticism."

This non-criticism, as such, begins raining down from all quarters, and usually comes in two forms:

(a) "Letting them sleep with you is wrong, because my sister did it, and her kid slept in bed with her until he was sixteen"; and

(b) "Letting them sleep with you is wrong, because my sister DIDN'T do it, and her kid has been sleeping alone since he was two months old. In fact, when he was a year old, he got his own apartment."

From the pile of baby books in the living room (which had now grown to such size that two different teams were scaling it, one from the north approach and one from the more treacherous but quicker Kitchen Side), two had emerged as leading contenders for our attention. One was from Kindly Doctor Sears, who says you need to hold the baby, sleep with the baby, wear the baby, be the baby, and all will be right with the universe, and man will lay down his sword and shield down by the riverside and study war no more.

The other was from Reality Doctor Ferber, who has trained parents in the fine art of Teaching Babies To Sleep since, I think, Wilma Flintstone was weaning Pebbles.

Our well-intentioned friends and relations usually got around to proffering advice on something called Ferberizing Max, which appears to go something like: Let him cry it out, a little at a time, until he falls asleep by himself, or collapses from exhaustion, or you collapse from exhaustion, or the social workers come and take the baby away for a while so you can get some sleep.

I tried it. I really did. We put Max in his crib, and he started crying, and I walked away, and let him cry, hoping he'd stop on his own.

I lasted all of 30 seconds.

We have lots of friends who made it through this process; they now sleep long hours, have well-adjusted children, and can face their futures (namely, the next 24 hours) with the gratifying knowledge that they won't have to excuse themselves from high-powered meetings to go take a nap.

Unfortunately, that was not us.

So, here's what we decided: We would let Max sleep in our bed—but only until he learned to talk, and could understand it when we talk.

Then we would bribe him, but good.

Actually, I had a lot of trouble imagining that Max would ever talk. He had one word, at this point: "Baaaw!" This was clearly an important point, because he repeated it often, usually at the highest decibel level he could muster, which was actually pretty impressive, considering he weighed only 20 pounds. Rachel was convinced he was saying "Ball," because a few times he said this when he saw the ball. I pointed out that he also said this when he saw the bottle, the bed, Mister Bumblebee, the car, the lamp, the Swiss cheese, the television, the jar of prunes and oatmeal, Daddy's head, and that yucky Balmex stuff you have to put on when you change their diapers and then can never get it off your fingers.

Rachel was undaunted: "Yes, but he ALWAYS says it when he sees the ball. He only USUALLY says it when he sees those other things." This is the logic that drove our lives.

If the truth be told, I must say that, between Max and our dog, Pearl, if I really had to assume one of them would gain the power of speech, I was ready to put my money on Pearl. Look, Pearl at least understood that words carry meaning: "Pearl, dinner?" "Treats!" "Walk?" "Down!" "Sit!" "Good dog!" "Go get *The New York Times*, but make sure it's the late edition." Pearl, you see, gets the word thing. So if she were to suddenly wish me a good day on my way out the door, I wouldn't be as surprised as if Max did it.

Max was a lovely, non-verbal being. I adored our non-verbal life together—I talked to him, like any dad does, but I know he understood the sound, the tone of voice, the smile, the touch, the clap of hands, the funny noise, and not really the words. That's fine. But talking? It didn't seem possible that he'd actually develop the ability to speak, any more than it was possible that the dishwasher would develop the ability to sing karaoke.

Still, he progressed and changed, each day, much, much faster than I could believe. I tried to live in the moment, not looking ahead to the changes to come, not looking back to the phases past—and yet, when I saw parents with a little three-month-old baby in a restaurant, I would turn to Rachel, and we sighed: "Oh, remember when Max was a baby?"

Because, at one year and change, he was not a baby any-more. This is very, very hard for the older dad. You've just gotten used to the baby thing—the feel of him, like a foot-ball under your arm, as you went about the shopping or the cleaning. The look of him, those innocent eyes, that great gaping-mouthed toothless smile that melted your heart. And now, you knew, because of your age, that you would never have that again. Yes, Rachel and I talked about it. We had created five embryos, implanted three, one took—meaning Max had two frozen brothers or sisters sitting in a tiny, tiny little frozen hotel in Arlington, Virginia, at the Institute for In-credibly Expensive Reproductive Alternatives. I was paying more per month to house them than a similar-sized room at the Ritz would have cost (considering that their room was one square inch; of course, the air conditioning bills were enormous. But then again, the room service was lousy). We talked about it, but we knew it would never happen. We couldn't go through it all again. A baby at fifty? Please. Forty-seven is one thing, but fifty?

Well, when you put it that way, there doesn't seem to be that much difference, does there? Still, we were resigned to our fate.

It was over.

And it was sad.

I missed having a baby.

I knew I would never have a baby again.

Fortunately, I had someone to take his place: This little child, this incredibly busy, active, wild child. Max suddenly had little time for lying in my arms and being rocked, as he had just a few months ago. He was like a hermit crab on crystal meth, scuttling across the floor with an acceleration rate that Detroit automakers only dream of, headed for his next appointment. He has magazines to rip up! Big sticks to put in his mouth! Electrical outlets to explore! Tupperware to toss! Cheerios to throw on the floor! Spit-up to distribute evenly among all of this father's articles of clothing! Telephones to gnaw! Ottomans to pull up on so he can fall on his head! Couches to fall off of! Chairs to topple! Balls to roll! Plates to send crashing off the table! Pens to insert into his ear! Dangerous kitchen implements to grab at! Garbage cans to knock over! Dogs to teethe on!

Until, finally, he falls asleep, exhausted, and we lie him in his crib, and he cries, and we take him in our arms, and bring him to bed. And he looks up at us, not sleeping, not playing, not crying, not crawling, not fussing—just looking at us, regarding us with his big brown eyes, a look of great import and intent.

Almost as though he has something he wants to say.

We tried to be as non-neurotic as parents can be, considering that parents are the most neurotic people on the face of the earth (and this comes from a man who has known many television personalities). We tried to stay calm, believing that Max picks up on our emotions, and that if we stayed calm, so would he.

Sometimes, this was not possible.

We took Max and Anna on a trip over the holidays to the Turks and Caicos Islands, because we figured, having a baby and a teenager wasn't enough stress—let's try international travel with lots of luggage through small airports between Christmas and New Year's.

We checked into our beautiful suite, a big bay window looking out on that pure azure Caribbean water the color of dreams, and sat out on the comfy chaise longues on our beautiful deck, and thought, you know, having a baby when you're older has some advantages. Who gets to cradle a baby in paradise like this? I could never have afforded this in my twenties. (Actually, I couldn't really afford it now, but you get better at deficit spending as you get older.)

Things were going fine.

Until one otherwise beautiful afternoon.

I was in the bedroom and I heard Rachel scream from the living room: "Phil! Come here! I need you right now! He can't breathe!"

I raced in from the bedroom. Max had spit up, and was choking, and could not get a breath. Rachel was in a panic.

From some very deep place, I remembered what to do, though I don't ever remember learning it. I reached a finger in, and cleared his airway, then turned him on my knee, and hit him hard with my palm on his back.

He started coughing, and screaming, and crying.

It was the most beautiful sound in the world.

But then he started spitting up blood.

All your fears—fears of being in a third world country when your child is in need of immediate medical attention—flood to the fore in a moment like this. And they all dissolved a minute later, after we called the front desk, when four hotel employees showed up with walkie-talkies. One of them had a doctor on a cell phone. They were smart and efficient and calm, and in that moment I loved them with all my heart and soul.

The doctor assured us, from listening to Max cry in the background, that he was in no danger. "Sir, if he's crying, he's breathing. That's a good thing." I agreed. It was a very, very, very good thing.

The hotel staff rushed us to the doctor's clinic, where he quickly determined that the blood had come only because I scratched Max's throat when I reached my finger in. Max, he said, was perfectly fine.

For Max, he prescribed nothing.

For me and Rachel, rum punches, immediately. (There are some good things about getting sick in the Caribbean.)

And so, I will admit, we became just a little bit more neurotic, jumping a little more whenever he coughed, keeping him a little closer to us.

And for the moment, we decided, if he wants to sleep next to us, and people think he shouldn't, well, we would leave that question for another moment.

For that night, we decided, we would just hold him as close as we possibly could.

❦

In the first year, there's not all that much difference between having a boy and a girl. In the next year, as the milestones start speeding by—look, Max can hold a sippy cup!
Max can walk! Max can do *The New York Times* crossword
puzzle! (OK, I did most of it, and he wasn't actually filling
in the squares as much as sleeping in my lap, but still.)—
you start looking at your friends with little girls, and yourself with a little boy, and it all starts to diverge.

And as time went on, I began to think that creationists
must all have girl children, because it's clear to anyone
who has a boy that we are, undoubtedly, descended from
monkeys.

I don't mean anything sexist by that—but anyone who
has a boy child has to live with one clear developmental
distinction. My friend Bill's daughter is two weeks older,
and already could count to 12—in Spanish. Max still hadn't
mastered "da-da," but he could go down a slide standing
up, better than any kid around.

Max was a relatively late walker, actually. But when he
got going, he got going. He started walking on a Wednesday; he started dancing on a Friday; and by the next Monday, he was engaged in his main form of entertainment:
Climbing Onto Dangerous Things. For months, Max actually did that dawn-of-man walk from *Planet of the Apes*.
Then suddenly he went upright, the better to reach precar-
ious perches. We were certain that, if a child's first words
are an imitation of the sounds he hears, then Max's first
words would be, "No! Get down from there!"

The talking thing was, we had to admit, a bit strange. Max
babbled incessantly, but there didn't seem to be any real

words in there. Most kids Max's age seemed to be starting to attach nouns to important objects (da-da, mommy, dog, bottle; the more precocious kids had graduated to words like "Barney," "cell phone," and "Porsche"). Max's peers also all seemed adept at that kiddie-quiz game that parents love, the one where you give really big hints (Parent: "What does a dog say? Does a dog say 'woof'? Is 'woof' what a dog says?" Child: "Woof." Parent: "Genius!").

Max, however, even failed this simple test—unless you accepted the idea that a dog says "Garruba no-no." If that's the case, then Max was brilliant.

As far as I could tell, Max had only a few real phrases. For one, he seemed insistent on telling the world that "Barabbas murdered Ronald Reagan!"—which is, of course, silly, because what could Barabbas possibly have against Ronald Reagan? He barely knew the man. Also, Max got quite worked up if you didn't pay attention to his warning, "Joe Biden go Baaden-Baaden! Joe Biden go Baaden-Baaden!" I guess if the senator from Delaware gets caught in a Euro-laundering scandal in Germany, we can't say Max didn't warn us.

When I would come home from work, Max would take my hand, lead me to the playroom, point to his box of stickers, and announce, "Ban the bomb!" I'm not sure what this early-sixties leftist slogan had to do with the stickers, but I played along, grabbing a nice doggy sticker for Max—which he proceeded to put on his nose, after which he hopped around the room doing the Sticker-Nose Dance, which I could only assume derived from early ban-the-bomb rallies.

There is little, however, one can do with this information, other than put a nice doggy sticker on your own nose and join in the Sticker-Nose Dance.

Proving, of course, what every teenager already knows: Parents are the dorkiest people in the universe. Poor Anna had to suffer through all of this, but at least she took respite in the main form of communication of all teenagers, which is to look at us, roll her eyes, and mutter, "whatever." I felt for her. I really did.

Since, here he was, two years old, and he still wasn't talking. And there were other oddities: He refused to relate to other children his age. And he still had the penchant for strange activities like putting his ear to the ground and wheeling his car back and forth in front of his face for an hour—you know, I tried it myself, it's very soothing, but putting it all together, the doctors started to get, as they so gently put it, concerned. They started using a euphemism so mild that you know it's hiding something just awful. They started raising the possibility that Max was on . . . The Spectrum. Not The Spectrum as in the old home of the Philadelphia 76ers, of course, although Max was showing an inordinately precocious talent for two-foot basketball; no, they were referring to a group of syndromes known as autistic spectrum disorders. Autism, it turns out, comes in many forms, all involving various kinds of problems with communication, language, and interpersonal skills. The doctors were raising the specter that perhaps Max had the mild form of autism known as Asperger's syndrome.

OK, guys, let's get this out of the way. It is pronounced "Ass-Burger." And yes, through all the proper concern a parent should have, and I did have, comes the one concern only a guy can have: Please, please, I don't want anything to be wrong with my baby, but if there is, I will do whatever he needs. Just don't let it be called Ass-burgers.

I shared this concern with no one. It's embarrassing.

But you wanted the truth.

Deeper down, though, my reaction was different than I thought it would be. My Grandma Fagel would faint if I had a hangnail, and I thought I would be the same way. But my love for Max, at this point, was so deep, so pure, so unassailable, so throw-yourself-in-front-of-a-truck, that I felt . . . calm. Max is Max, I thought. Whatever he is, he is, and whatever he needs, we will try to provide, but call it what you will—call it Shitfuckpiss Picklenose syndrome, for all I care. He is my son, and I love him, and nothing else matters.

Isn't that a pisser? That's what you feel.

It makes you feel very strong, to feel this way.

It makes you feel . . . like a Man.

Because, in this moment—this moment of facing your greatest fears about your child and knowing there's really not much you can do about them—in this moment you realize it's not about putting bad guys behind bars, it's not about control, it's not about having people do what you tell them to do, it's not about finding order in the universe. It's all just about being In This Moment, facing it, accepting it, accepting that you are who you are, and your child is who he is, and there's not much more to it than that, other than (kina horah) the fact that with any luck you may get to wake up with each other for years in the world—that's what it means to be a Man.

I felt like a Non-Action Hero.

And it felt right.

Not that we just sat around and did nothing, of course. As a precaution, we started taking Max to a speech therapist, because, well, this is what you do.

Going to a speech therapist consisted of us watching through a two-way mirror as a nice lady with big teeth said things to Max.

Very.

Clearly.

And.

Very.

Slowly.

Things like: "Max, should we OH-pen the box? Would you like to OH-pen the box? Can you say OH? If you say OH we can OH-pen the box!" After a half an hour of this, Max had clearly had enough. He tried to get the heck out of there, but the door was shut.

I will give him this, though—he pointed to the door, looked at the lady, and, in as sarcastic a voice as a two-year-old can muster, said simply, "OH."

I thought, hey, it's a start.

The problem was not that Max didn't understand words, mind you. It was quite astounding, in fact, when you said something like "Max, can you go pick a pepperoni off Anna's pizza for Daddy," and he did it, and you wondered, when did he learn the word "pepperoni"? Or "pizza"? Or, for that matter, "Anna"? One minute, you say, "Here, Max, hand this ball to Anna," and instead, he throws it in the garbage. And the next day, you say, "Max, can you find Daddy's shoes?" And without hesitation, he goes into the closet and finds your shoes.

And throws them in the garbage.

So we waited for the speech to come, and in the meantime ranged between astounded and dumbfounded at the leaps of cognition that came each day: His love of Elmo (whom he called "Bubba"), his ability to dance to the beat of his favorite band, The Wiggles (all of whom he called "Bubba,") his delight when he would see himself ("Bubba") in the mirror.

Overall, the talking thing was not our main concern, at this stage in his development. Everything else in the realm of cognition seemed to be falling into place. He had an easy laugh and a great sense of humor (his best joke was falling off the bed. He seemed to think that was REALLY funny), he loved to play with his daddy (or anybody, for that matter, as long as he wasn't left without entertainment for more than forty seconds), and, as I mentioned, he could dunk a basketball like nobody's business (if there were only a two-foot-basket league, we could retire right then and there).

The big problem, if we're being honest, was something none of the baby books warned us about.

It all started just after Rachel weaned him, at about 19 months. It was a decision we made carefully, deliberately, and after much serious thought ("Honey, I had too many Rum and Cokes tonight. Maybe he shouldn't breast-feed anymore." We considered this a sound medical decision, because we were out drinking with a doctor.).

It was shortly after we got home, about three one morning, when Max, who was in our bed (yes, he was STILL sleeping with us; those who had been saying "I told you so" when we let Max sleep in our bed as a baby were now doing the full I-told-you-so dance)—anyway, it was three in the morning, and I was awakened by the dulcet tones of my lovely wife, screaming, "Max! Ow! Let go of Mommy's boobie!"

It is in these moments that men learn what marriages are made of, because, if you laugh, as is your wont to do, you will lose valuable Husband Points, which, given the current state of the Who's Getting Up With The Baby In The Middle of The Night contest, you sorely cannot afford. And so you stifle your sleepy giggles, and begin thinking of how you're going to tell this story at work the next day.

But if I knew then what I know now, I would not have been chuckling into my pillow.

Because that night was the beginning of The Nipple Wars.

Now, before I continue, let me say that "nipple" is not a word that men use easily. It's not a dirty word, per se, but for some reason, guys who have no trouble using the F-word as a noun, verb, and adjective in the same sentence, stumble over "nipple." It's like "panties." Or "uvula."

The Nipple Wars would commence each night just as Max was falling asleep. He would—I kid you not—reach up under Rachel's shirt until he found the source of his former sustenance, and begin to pinch as hard as he could.

For several nights, I continued to find this hysterical.

Until it was my turn to put him to bed.

And he started doing it to me.

We were just finishing up our books, which I change the words of to keep myself from getting bored ("One fish, two fish, goy fish, Jew fish"), and we were through with our bottle, and the lights were off, and Max was beginning to nod off—and slowly, slowly, a hand was crawling up under my T-shirt, headed straight for a nipple. He grabbed on, and delivered a pinch that—well, let me just say, I got in a fight with Alan Cohen in the fourth grade over some baseball cards, and he used the same move, and to this day, he still has my Tom Tresh Rookie Special.

So, I gently moved Max's hand away, and stroked his head, softly, to help him drift off to sleep.

And he began screeching.

Nothing—I mean nothing, even my best version of "Yes Sir, That's My Baby," the song I had been singing to him since the womb—nothing could quiet him down. Until I let him squeeze the appendage in question, again. And he immediately began drifting off to sleep.

Now, any parent out there understands this dilemma: Move his hand away, teach him a lesson, and know he will not fall asleep for hours? Or endure 30 seconds of unendurable agony, watch your toddler drift off to sleep, and go watch *The Sopranos?*

Well, about 30 seconds later, as I picked up my sleeping angel in one arm, and massaged my aching breast with the other, I carried Max off to his crib, and realized what so many parents before me knew all too well:

This baby stuff carries with it enormous pleasure, and enormous pain.

Often at the same time.

I guess I'm just lucky to learn it so soon.

But it is not the nights that predominate my thoughts at this juncture. It is the mornings. The mornings, when we hear Max's voice over the monitor, babbling away to his pillow that's shaped like a moon with a smiley face, a long dissertation filled with words that sound like nonsense to me but I'm sure hold great meaning, and I walk into his room, and he looks up and smiles at me, and raises his arms to be lifted from his crib, and I lift him still clutching Mister Moon, and I hold him, warm and soft and relaxed, his hand patting my cheek, exploring my ears, resting on my shoulder; and we raise the shades, and look out the window on the most glorious of mornings, glorious because I have this moment, this incredible moment, groundhog running by the country stream, this must be the day that all of my dreams come true—so happy just to see you smile, underneath this sky of blue, on this new morning, new morning, on this new morning with you.

So, happy birthday, Max. Now you are two. I guess the biggest milestone was last Saturday night—Mom has to go to New York next week, and we're not sure how you'll make it through a night without her, so we decided I would solo for a night (with Mom sleeping upstairs with Anna, just in case). I put you to bed, as I do every night, and you woke up at 12:23 a.m., as you do just about every night—it's weird, really, how accurate you can be—and I actually got you back to sleep without Mom. Once, anyway. You woke up again at 3 a.m., and started crying inconsolably, and I didn't know what to do. I held you and rocked you and sang to you, and you screamed and you screamed and you

screamed. I almost went and got your mom. But first, I took you in the bathroom and turned on the shower, and the sound and the warmth of it calmed you down, and when you'd stopped crying I took you into bed with me, and you fell fast, fast asleep, and we held each other all night. And in the morning, you woke up smiling and happy, and we just cuddled, and tickled, and sang, and you babbled and babbled, your little nonsense soliloquy I've come to live for. Eventually we got up, and I got you and me dressed, and we went down to breakfast, and a little later Mommy came down—but for one night, for one morning, you were all mine, all mine, all mine. And if you never speak a coherent word, I will understand anyway, because on this night, you came to me in silent whispers and told me all that any father will ever need to know.

Thank you for that.

6

Neuroses Are Red

Fuck.

Fuck fuck fuck.

Fuck!

Fuck! Fuck! Fuck! Fuck! Fuck!

Fuck!

Shit.

Fuck this shit.

Fuckita-fuckita-fuckita-fuckita-fuckita-fuckita-fuckita-fuckita.

OK, thanks for letting me get that off my chest. When there's a four-year-old around, of course, you have to be very, very careful, because they repeat everything you say, especially if you accidentally curse in front of them—not like a little echo chamber, but like a computer virus. They store it up, secretly and silently and undetected on their hard drives, and then, at the most inopportune moment—say, for example, when you're meeting with the rabbi to discuss enrolling Max in the Shlomo Raven Day Care Center—it pops up. So it's in your best interest to learn to stifle the curses.

But each time you stifle yourself, of course, the curse doesn't go away, whenever you hit your thumb, or lock the keys in the car, or stub your toe, or drop your cell phone in the toilet, and you manage to transmute your reflex curse on its way from the brain to the mouth, so it comes out "Oh, fuuuuuu . . . lis Navidad!" Or you invent your own curses, like W. C. Fields—in the days before you could say "God damn" in a movie, he would trip over a log or break a mirror, or a child would kick him in the shins, and he'd mutter, "GODfry DANiels," and get that past the censors. (Those days have returned, by the way—at *America's Most Wanted*, we had to run our scripts past what is euphemistically known as "Network Standards and Practices," as though Fox actually had any standards. You've seen what you can do on TV these days—you can make people eat worms, drop them off of tall buildings, and show an entire woman's body except, apparently, for Janet Jackson's right nipple, but you cannot say "God" and "damn" in the same sentence. Interestingly, they made us bleep the "God" but let us leave in the "damn." As though God were the curse word. It seemed strange, but hey, it made them happy, and we got to drop more people off of tall buildings.)

The point being, when you stifle curses, they don't go away. They just build up inside, and if you don't let them out occasionally, in a safe place, your head explodes.

This is what Dads' Night Out is for.

As the room dad in Max's preschool, I am in charge of many very important activities, including bringing the donuts for Daddy Day—when all the dads come to school for an hour before going to the office, and stand around like schmucks in suits drinking coffee from tiny Styrofoam cups in the playground, watching our kids scream at each other until it's time to join the exciting Daddy-Child Activity of taking a big wooden letter of your child's first initial and painting it blue. I am also in charge of arranging Dads' Night Out, when we could, in theory, bond over the important child-rearing issues of the day, including how to get the blue paint off your good shoes.

There was actually a lot less cursing than I expected on Dads' Night Out. The dads mostly seemed to just enjoy the ability to finish a sentence—because when you have a four-year-old, it's pretty tough to get a word in edgewise. Just this morning, Max was giving a dissertation on dinosaurs.

"Dad, when the meteorite hit the earf, all the dinosaurs had to go away, but before that, there were dinosaurs, and did you know that a Tyrannosaurus rex can eat a Saltopus?"

I had no idea what a Saltopus was, but I wasn't going to tell him that.

"A Tyrannosaurus rex is the biggest dinosaur," I began to say, in that lilting voice we dads use to make everything we say sound both important, interesting, and fun.

Guess what. Our teenager has figured out already that parents are neither important, interesting, nor fun; but I didn't realize that the knowledge started back at age four.

Max didn't even let me finish the sentence. "No no no," Max insisted. "Patasaurus is the biggest dinosaur. He has a long neck, so he can eat the leaves off the tall trees. The tall trees, Dad. Dad! The tall trees! He has to eat the leaves off the tall trees! Daaaaad!"

OK, first of all, did you know that they don't call them brontosaurus anymore? Turns out the scientists who named the dinosaurs when we were kids were all C students, or stoned, because the next generation came along and said, no no no, you have all the heads on the wrong bodies, and switched everything around and gave them more scientifically appropriate but less daddy-used-to-know-this names.

But having a four-year-old correct you is only half the problem with kids learning to speak.

The other half is Dora.

Dora the Explorer is the most popular cartoon on the planet these days. It is so politically correct that even Al Gore can't watch it. Dora speaks both English and Spanish, which is very cool, but this is not:

She says everything like *THIS!* And *SO* does everyone on her *SHOW!* They have all the child actors sound really excited at the *END* of their *SENTENCES!* You can watch Dora *MANY* times *EVERY DAY!* And so this *NEVER* fucking *ENDS!* Sorry, I mean it *NEVER* Far-Rockaway *ENDS!*

And what's worse, she's obnoxious in English *AND SPANISH!* Sí! Es malsonante en *inglés Y ESPAÑOL!*

And before you know it, your *KID* starts talking *LIKE THIS!* All *DAY!*

And so do *YOU!*

So for a chance to speak in complete sentences and a normal tone of voice, with people vaguely our own age and sex, and with about our own amount of misinformation about dinosaurs, I led the class fathers off to Dads' Night Out.

I decided we should go to Ruth's Chris Steak House, since ordering a steak the size of your head seemed like the manly thing to do (and by the way, is Ruth's Chris the dumbest name for a restaurant ever? Turns out the woman who bought Chris's Steak House in New Orleans back in 1965 was actually pretty cool. Three months after she mortgaged her house to buy the place, Hurricane Betsy tore up the Gulf Coast, and knocked out the power to New Orleans. Instead of just losing the thousands of pounds of beef that were getting warm in her meat lockers, she cooked steaks all day over a gas stove and served them free to relief and emergency workers. Neat lady, but hey, either leave it as Chris's, or put your name on it. She apparently couldn't decide, so she went with Ruth's Chris Steak House. I have trouble eating at places with bad names—I can't even walk into a Chick-fil-A—but for the sake of fatherly unity and giant slabs of meat, I put that aside for the night).

As we hacked away at our cow-sized dinners, and I did my best Art Linkletter imitation, leading the dads through a session of *Kids Say the Darndest Things* (apparently Linkletter wanted to call his early-sixties TV show *"Kids Say the God-Darndest Things,"* but the censors nixed that), and I was telling about how Max corrects me in everything these days—"No, Daddy, it's not a banister, I call it a railing"—and how I have to watch my cursing because he repeats everything I say, and how, in order to speak to my wife for a minute, we have to tell Max, "Honey, please stop talking for one minute, Daddy needs to ask Mommy where the car keys are" ("No no no Daddy! Daddy doesn't talk now! I'm talking! I have to tell you . . . my blue race car is the fastest in the whole world!")

. . . and I found myself drifting off, which I'll tend to do anyway after three glasses of wine these days, but this was different; I was drifting into that strange place fathers find themselves, confronted with the contradictions that are brought on by time: How very strange it is, after such a long time of worrying that a child would never speak, to be telling him to Shut The Fu . . . uuuu . . . linni Movie.

I certainly could never have imagined, just after Max's second birthday, that I would ever tell him to shut up. As I've said, he still hadn't even called me da-da yet. We were still facing the fear of Asperger's syndrome. My nipples were purple from getting pinched every night.

And there were other worries. It was around this time, when Max was two years and a bit, that I became obsessed with the dad's next great fear:

Honey, I lost the kid.

Granted, as someone who has worked with the parents of missing children for 15 years, I am particularly prone to this fear. Neither John Walsh nor I went through a single day in all those years without getting a call from a tearful and frantic parent. It has to get to you. Oddly, on those occasions when I'd be out in a public place with John Walsh and his kids, I felt a peculiar calm—John, the most famous father of a missing child ever, didn't hover over his kids, didn't freak out when they left his sight, didn't sweat it when they left us at a ballgame to go get a hot dog. I asked him how he could possibly stay so calm, and he said it was because he'd taught his kids the rules, and knew they knew how to handle themselves.

Only now, when Max was an ambulatory but non-verbal two-year-old, did I get it: Of course. Walsh's children were over four years old when I met them. They had passed through the stage of lunacy when children are, I am convinced, incapable of learning anything, including how not to get lost.

Don't worry—I never actually did lose Max. Not even close. This, however, did not keep me from experiencing, several times a day, the neurotic, testicle-clenching fear— "Omigod where is he? Max! Oh, there he is, sitting in my lap. Phew!"

I remember the first time I really did take Max to Starbucks with me, back when he was a baby. He had one of those enormously complex devices known to all parents as the Snap N Go (called such because the name Fight-With-The-Crying-Child-To-Get-Into-It, Catch-Your-Finger-In-The-Slot-As-You-Try-To-Put-The-Seat-In-The-Car, Scream-Bloody-Murder-And-Go—while more accurate— was already taken). I did what all dads do—put my Mint Mocha Macchiato on top of the car, took the Snap-And-Go, along with little Max, out of the stroller, clicked it into its little docking device in my backseat, and drove off with the coffee on the roof.

And then, the fear. Wait—did I just put the coffee in the seat and Max on the roof? Oh my God!

Because when the kid is in that little Snap N Go basket, you do tend to set him down once in awhile—to get your keys, scratch your butt, whatever. And let's face it, as you approach fifty, everything else you set down gets lost sooner or later—keys, glasses, coffee, books, wallets, drinks, light-bulbs, magazines, dogs, cats, BMWs—what's to stop you from setting Max down on the counter at the drugstore and walking away?

I am truly sorry if this thought has not occurred to you.

Because once you have thought it, you cannot unthink it. Ever.

For months after that, I was obsessed with the fear that I would leave that little apple basket someplace, with Max in it. I would be driving along, and an electric shock would run through me—Oh my God! Did I put Max in the car? And I would whip around, and there he would be, face-backward, my little turtle in his plastic-and-foam-pillow shell, completely absorbed in another attempt to fit both feet in his mouth simultaneously.

So by the time Max had turned two, and was walking, my fear of losing him had had a good long time to simmer and develop into a full-fledged neurosis.

I will share with you my most embarrassing example, because I am a father and therefore devoid of pride: Now that Max's car seat was forward-facing, I loved to drive along in the convertible and, when there were no cars behind us, tilt my rearview mirror down for a minute, so I could see him and he could see me, and we would giggle at each other, and I would smile with my eyes, and he would get that, and laugh, and shake a toy truck at me. And then I'd return the mirror to its normal position, to check for cars behind me.

And then I'd drive, and forget I'd done that.

And I'd look in the rearview mirror.

And I'd only see empty road.

No Max.

GONE!

Max was gone!

Holy shit, he flew out of the car! The top is open! Oh God in heaven! Noooo! Max! I—oh, right, the mirror.

And I'd adjust it down, and there was Max, and he would catch my eye, and smile, and wave a toy truck at me.

This only happened, I will say, two or three times.

A day.

Dads are stupid like that.

I can see, now, that the fear of losing Max was all part of this process I was going through—moving from that place of total control over my life, my environment, my employees, my world, and the world of criminals and victims, to a place where I relinquished control, where—as the AA people say—I "let go and let God." Or, like the AAA people say, "Trust us, we'll be there within sixty minutes," or the AARP people, who say "Trust us, you're too old to handle things yourself."

It's all about trust, isn't it. The Greyhound people say "leave the driving to us," and the Allstate people say "you're in good hands," and the Audi people say "Vorsprung durch Technik"—well, I'm not sure that last one applies, but still, all these ads and groups and collectives created to tell us to try to stop trying to be in control, but it's so hard for a normal person, let alone a TV producer, to let go. (The most accurate of all film portrayals of TV producers, the majority of which are astoundingly unflattering—not necessarily unfairly, mind you, but astoundingly unflattering nonetheless—is Holly Hunter's character in *Broadcast News*, incapable of giving a cab driver a destination without telling him which route to take. We're all like that. Only worse. Don't ever ask a producer for directions to a restaurant. He's certain to say, "That restaurant is terrible! Why would you eat there? Let me tell you where to eat. . . . ")

The fear of losing Max was omnipresent. I'd be putting the groceries in the trunk, and he'd walk around the car, and

I'd walk around after him a moment later, and—he was gone! Max! MAAAX! Oh my God! Dial 911! MAAAX!—until a kindly passerby would point out that he'd just walked around to the other side of the car. And I would pick him up and hug him, tears squeezing out of my eyes, and I wanted to make him promise to never walk out of my sight ever, ever again; maybe, I actually thought, I should just keep him in the house until he learns to talk, so he can promise me that.

Until he can say, I won't get lost, Daddy.

Until he can say, trust me.

He of course could not say that yet. But he was, finally, starting to speak.

Sort of.

His little vocabulary of mispronounced but distinct words grew daily—and when we'd go out at night, we had to leave babysitters with a Max–English dictionary, so they'd know what the hell he was talking about. He called himself "baby," for some reason, rather than Max. "Baby won meezees" meant Max wanted music; "Baby see garbo tots" meant either that he had seen a garbage truck, or Greta Garbo's tits. Cookies were tee-tees, cars were hars, more was moin, coming was timin. "Moin warran tots timin" meant more orange trucks were coming, and "baby won moin tome" meant Max wanted another ice cream cone.

But we were not merely the anthropologists studying this strange dialect; we were also slaves to it. The speech therapists insisted that, if he got what he wanted when he used words, then he'd be inclined to use them more often.

I don't know how he managed to pay her to say that. But I'm sure he did.

Because, suddenly, our days were consumed in carrying out the orders of Professor Irwin Corey. "Tee-tee! Moin! Moin!" he would shout, and we would scurry for the counters and cupboards in search of more Oreo tee-tees, certain that if we did not provide a positive reinforcement for the language, the language would be lost. It was a simple Skinnerian exercise in behavior modification.

But as so often happens in science, we were oblivious to the fact that it was we, not Max, who were the subjects of the experiment: One word from our mumble-mouthed lab rat and it was we who would salivate, desperately trying to find our way through the maze of words to figure out what the heck he was asking for. "Pete Dodurt"—a pink yogurt! "Pop-pop"—a lollypop! "Blue one"—a pacifier! (That was a toughie. Like the way *The New York Times* crossword gets harder as the week goes by, so did Max's puzzles.)

But would that the edicts of Max's speech therapist ended there.

No, my friends, that wasn't the worst of it.

The worst—well, you know, we've come this far together, and I've used some rough language, and so if you're still with me, I think I may have earned your trust somewhat, but I'm going to put that all on the line, right now, because I am going to tell you something that will strike fear into the hearts of any self-respecting father. If you leave me right now, I will understand. But I've vowed to make this memoir as honest as possible, and so I must say it, straight out: I must tell you what our next orders were.

We had to give up television.

All of it. DVDs, videotapes, Saturday-morning cartoons.

I can feel your shudders of revulsion and fear. Because we all know that once they start walking, you have two choices: Devote your every waking moment to following them around, rendering second-by-second judgments on the safety of various activities ("That's good Max. Pat the dog. Yes, Max, that's nice how you're gentle with the dog. No, Max, you may not put your dinosaur in Pearl's poopy-hole. She doesn't like that. No, Max, you can't put it in your poopy-hole either. You won't like that. No, Daddy's is out altogether.")—or you can plop them down in front of *The Wiggles*, and have a half-hour to get the dishes done or put in a load of laundry.

All right, I mean read the Arts and Leisure section from last Sunday. But you get the point.

I remember back in my hippie days, when parents would try to raise children without television. It was fortunate that we were hippies, because raising children without television meant you had no time to, say, bathe, which somehow we felt was an unnatural activity anyway (boy, you know, we must have been really, really stoned to come up with some of this stuff). They were Parents Without Pause, there for their children every waking moment, and then some.

I remember those parents fondly.

God bless them for trying.

I visit them in the insane asylum on important holidays, like Abbie Hoffman's birthday.

No, that hippie holdover philosophy went out the window as soon as I discovered the 22 minutes of peace offered by *Go, Diego, Go!*

One other hippie holdover philosophy did affect me greatly, however, as Max passed through this year of his life:

the question of how to feed your child. I lived in Ithaca, New York, after I got out of college—one of the great hippie holdout communities in America. I went there last year, and guess what? Remember when the radicals took over the Cornell campus in the sixties, to protest the war? Turns out, they forgot to give it back. Or the rest of the town, either. Ithaca remains the most tie-dyed, long-haired, laid-back, Deadhead, toke-a-skinny, Hesse-reading, Phish-loving town in America, a place where culture stretches from James Dean to Howard Dean and back again; the home of the Moosewood Restaurant, the first place in America to ban smoking and have on the menu—and this was one of their most popular items—Steamed Trees and Dirt. Molly Katzen's *Moosewood Cookbook* just went into (I looked it up) its nine millionth edition. Buoyed along in my tofu salad days by this wave of healthy eating, I did hope to raise a child untainted by the rush and fall brought on by refined sugar, a child made mellow through a life lived in harmony, the energy flowing through his chakras unstemmed by the blockages caused by Cocoa Puffs and Kix.

But, as the Swami Satchidananda used to tell us: Fat Fucking Chance, Bub.

(Actually, I was quite a follower of Sri Swami Satchidananda back in the day, and I can still quote his great teachings: "You are born as the image of happiness, and you are happiness still. True and lasting happiness can only come from within. It can never come from anything you search for outside yourself. Except for a nice slice of pizza. That would really make me happy, right about now.")

It was easy to keep Max eating healthy when it was all baby food (or to be more accurate, baby food and television;

we'd prop him up in front of Baby Mozart, and his jaw would go slack, like Al Bundy watching "Girls Gone Wild: The Vatican," and we'd spoon some strained peas in there, and start his jaw moving, and Max would do the rest, which, basically, consisted of involuntarily swallowing to the beat of "Eine kleine Nachtmusik"). But now that he was eating real food, the challenge was much greater. As bad as his language was, he managed a firm "No deebee!" for no green beans, "No tarra" for no carrots, and "no fing dis no tee!" for Nothing That's Not A Cookie. Turns out that moment on their first birthday, when, after a year of nothing but mother's milk, you give them a bite of birthday cake? Yeah, that was the big mistake. A little seed was planted in their heads at that moment—well, that's a bad analogy, because this has nothing to do with seeds or anything else found in nature. Let's say they broke ground for a little Hostess Twinkie factory in their brains at that moment—and now, a little more than a year later, they can smell an alphabet cookie a mile away, and tell you which letter it is with their eyes closed.

Once again, your fading belief that you can Control Things comes to the fore, and you believe, with all your heart and your hippie soul, that you can psych this little toddler out. ("Toddler" is such an odd word, isn't it? The verb, "to toddle," means both to walk in an unsteady manner, and to walk in a leisurely way—which is why it can be applied both to your child and the entire town of Chicago. "That toddlin' town" is the most famous reference to the word in song, but the worst, and the oddest, is John Sebastian— in "Darling, Be Home Soon," it unfortunately mars one of the prettiest songs he ever wrote:

Darling be home soon
I couldn't bear to wait an extra minute if you dawdled
My darling be home soon
It's not just these few hours,
But I've been waiting since I toddled
For the great relief of having you to talk to

Toddled? Nobody uses "toddle" as a verb, let alone in the past tense. "Hey, Johnny started to toddle yesterday!" "He did? He toddled?" "Yes, yes, much toddling.")

The fact that men cannot accept what is, but must always try to repair, replace, renew, rewire, revamp, reallocate, reconnect—must always try to resomething—is both what makes us better parents than women, and more neurotic. Men cannot accept that they are helpless or useless against a problem. We say things like "there MUST be an answer" in situations when, clearly, there is not. And so I came to believe that our banning of the videos must have led to Max talking. It was equally possible that it was all a matter of chance and timing, but dads can never believe that. They must strive, again and again, tinkering and adjusting, try to fix their children, even when they're not broken. All of us who thought our fathers were disappointed in us, and who spent years in therapy trying to resolve our issues with our fathers, didn't realize: They were just tinkering with our carburetors, trying to get a little better mileage out of us.

Learning not to tinker—learning to accept, learning to say "it is what it is"—comes in waves, in stages, in fits and starts. Because the need to get in there and repair is deep-seated.

Again, women are like God in these matters. They don't have to continue to perform miracles. When you think about

God, you don't look at the guy who brought light in the firmament of heaven to divide the night and the day, freed the Jews from bondage, and created Raquel Welch, and say, yeah, but what have you done for me lately? So he's not under as much pressure as the rest of us dads, whose only tangible contribution thus far was figuring out how to assemble the Pack N Go.

So I continued to prove my worth by focusing on food; getting Max to eat anything besides crap became my struggle, as I continued to try to psych Max out. "Hey Max, look! Special treats today! Mommy bought *prunes*! Yay!" But they're way ahead of you. A prune is not ice cream. Ice cream is ice cream. This simple tautology drove our days. Max, I say, you can't have a cookie until you take two bites of your apple. Dad, he responds, you are creating a false order, and did not the guru Sachidananda tell us that false order is the path to darkness, and does not the word "guru" itself mean "remover of darkness?" So will you please remove this darkness from my soul and give me the damned cookie?

We struggled, every day, every night, every meal, every bite. Remember my wife's sociobiological argument about why guys are prone to cheat? She says it explains why kids crave sugar. It was the cavemen with the sweet-tooth gene who ate the ripest fruits, and therefore had the energy to outrun the mastodons. It certainly seemed like an urge that dated back to caveman times, because when I would deny Max the sweets he demanded, he would hit me with a club.

Not only was it harder to get Max to eat, now that we had given up television—but everything else in our lives seemed to get harder, too. Without a good 22-minute Baby Van Gogh to plant him in front of, we had a lot less time to run the household.

This is the time you have to teach your wife football.

Specifically, the difference between zone defense and man-to-man.

Let's say she's paying bills at the dining room table, for example, while I'm cooking dinner. Max is running a down-and-out pattern toward the lamp. There are two ways to handle this: You go man-to-man, in which case either the bills don't get paid or dinner doesn't get cooked, because one of you is devoted to Max Defense. Or you can play zone: I cook until Max comes into the kitchen, you pay bills until Max comes into the dining room.

This saved us. It really did. Rachel got very good at it, although when Max would run the counter-trey, we had to go into nickle-prevent, and have Anna come downstairs to cover the deep-corner bathroom.

But it was of limited effectiveness. Now that the television was gone, our entire existence began to disintegrate: Max was eating nothing but whipped cream. The house was a disaster, since no one had time to clean. We smelled terrible, since days would go by between showers. Shingles fell from a neglected roof, shutters loosed from their hinges banged in the wind, cats howled, coyotes roamed the living room, the cars stopped running, snow blew in through gaping holes in the walls, cavemen banged their clubs on the kitchen table protesting their overuse in sociobiological metaphors, bands of youths in gang-color bandanas patrolled the hallways demanding money for cigarettes. . . .

But it was all worth it.

Because Max learned to talk.

Star! Moon! he said, pointing to the night sky. Da-da! he said, pointing to me. "Big Ball!" he said, pointing to my belly (well, you gain weight when you have a kid. It's inevitable). One! Two! Three! Cup! Fish! Wa-wa! With each word, a look of both satisfaction and astonishment would cross his face, as if to say, oh, is this what you were waiting for? Why didn't you say so?

He sat down on the potty. "Peeee!" He got in the bath. "Momma duck! Baby duck! Momma duck kiss baby duck!" He got out of the bath. He looked at his hand. "Hand!" A slow survey of the rest of his little, beautiful, naked self. "Foot!" "Arm!" "Two foot!"

In a matter of days, it was all over. The Year of Pretending Not to Be Nervous About Max's Lack Of Speech drew to a close, to the sounds of "Da-da, airplane!" and "Da-da, duck!" and, of course, the inevitable, "Da-da, excuse me, can we please end this sordid experiment and put a video on? I really would like to see what's been happening with poor Dorothy The Dinosaur. Did she ever find her rosy tea?"

We had been released, finally, from our fear that he would never speak. We had (I could convince myself) Solved The Problem, or (as Rachel suspected but never told me, because I was, after all, a Man, who could not grasp the concept) The Problem Had Worked Itself Out By Itself Irrespective Of Anything We Had Done.

Suddenly, this child who was nearly two-and-a-half years old, and this man who was forty-eight-and-a-half, were having conversations. Chats. And, of course, arguments. "Max, time for dinner." "One more minute! Play one more minute!" he would shout. "Max, time to go to bed." "One more minute!" How did speech go from something so devoutly to be wished, to something so devoutly annoying? And yet . . .

. . . at night, I would put him in his pajamas ("Baby put on jamas!"), and ask him what we do next ("Brush ow teet!"), and read him his books ("four books, da-da! Read four books!"), astounded, at each turn, that these words came tumbling out—and then we would turn off the light, and cuddle, and I would sing our songs (an off-key croon by me of "Yes, sir, that's my baby, no sir, don't mean maybe, yes, sir," and the heart-stoppingly incredible response from Max: "Dat my baby noooow!"); and one night, as I got up to go, Max uttered the most beautiful five words I have ever heard in my life: "Da-da cuddle one more minute."

Now, you're going to call me an idiot for saying this, and you will be absolutely correct, but here it is: Friends had warned me not to press too hard for Max to speak, because the loss of that lovely, non-verbal bond is an irrevocable one, and one that you will miss more than you can imagine. I thought it a ridiculous concept, and yet, there it was: As thrilled as I was to see his language finally emerging, I was also, once again . . .

. . . just a little sad. That life we had lived together—a life of grunts and smiles, of tickles and touches, when he spoke the world in silent whispers, was disappearing, like a dream; and like a dream, it was already becoming hard to remember, just days behind me and already a million miles away. I had seen it in other parents, and had guarded against it: I had videotaped, chronicled, journaled, recorded, edited, preserved in amber everything I could of that life and now, already, it seemed to have vanished in the haze. Already, this new life, this new communication, was erasing the old tapes, and all I could do was wave bye-bye.

At least, he was speaking now. I had to admit I was relieved to have that fear behind us. But in parenthood, as in any other good horror movie, when one terror is defeated, there's always another terror coming—and, as in any good horror movie, as soon as one of the principals says, "Well, we're safe now," you can go ahead and cue the Bernard Herrmann music, because the next attack is right around the corner.

These attacks came in the horrendous, addicting form of something known as The Milestone Chart.

The Millstone Chart would be a better name for it, because they hang around the daddy's neck like a great weight. The lessons we are trying to learn: to accept what is for what it is, to not try to Fix Everything, to love unconditionally like a mother, to not try to open the hoods and adjust the carburetors—these lessons are destroyed by the dreaded Milestone Charts.

I think when we were growing up we had more freedom simply because our parents didn't know what we were Supposed To Be Doing. That five-year-old who's still in diapers? Yeah, I think Yussel next door was the same way. He'll grow out of it. The seven-year-old kid who hasn't left his room yet? Shy. The one who hits all the other kids with a stick? Athletic.

But they didn't have the advantage of the Milestone Chart. Not only are these charts in every book (our book pile, by this point, having been zoned commercial; two Starbucks and a Baby Gap had opened near the south corner), but there are services now to e-mail you every week to tell you what your kid should be doing and isn't.

Tell me that's not enough to drive a dad insane.

There is no behavior too small to warrant note. When should a kid be able to turn the pages of a book? Sixteen months. Pedal a tricycle? Eighteen months. Make a tower of four blocks? Two years. Draw a vertical line? Two and a half. Use prepositions? Two months shy of three years.

Talk about having it down to a science. A terrible, guilt-inducing science. We had one book that told us what milestones to expect every *day*. "If your child is 274 days old today, expect him or her to begin waving bye-bye. Probably around 4 p.m. this afternoon or, for the more advanced child, 3:30."

There was one milestone Max was almost on time with, no thanks to us: It is the most life-changing moment in a parent's existence (until, a few years later, when you get the kid to mow the lawn. There is nothing as gratifying as doing the *Times* crossword while looking out the window and watching a child mowing a lawn in the hot sun. What's a four-letter word for ruler? Ah, yes. King.).

This moment was just as liberating.

Because Max had learned to use the potty.

Now, I will warn you. Everybody whose kid learns to use the potty, which, for the most part, is everybody, eventually, says, "the kid's potty-trained now," as though training has anything to do with it.

Which is, of course, another way parents delude themselves into thinking they have control of things they have no control over. It's the parental equivalent of going outside in a thunderstorm and shouting, "Stop raining!" and then, that afternoon, when the sun comes out, saying, "Well, I guess that did the trick." We, like any dutifully neurotic parents, looked at the Milestone Chart, found out it was three days until Max was due to be potty-trained, and started our potty training in earnest, which consisted of sitting Max on the potty.

And waiting.

Of all the boring moments of parenthood, and there are many, sitting on the bathroom floor and watching your child not pee is right up there with . . . well, no, I guess this is number one, until you get to third grade and the violin recitals start. I have spent more interesting hours at the DMV (where at least, every once in a while, someone goes postal because they spent two hours in the wrong line, and you get to watch the security guards decide whether they get to use their new Tasers). Here, there's just Max, not peeing, and then not peeing some more, and every once in awhile you turn on a faucet, or tell the story of Mister Fire Hose Saves The Day (Don't worry about the fire! Mister Fire Hose Is Here! "Pisssshhhhhhh!" Says Mister Fire Hose. "Pishhhhh! Pishhh! Pisssshhhhh!" And everybody cheered!)—all to no avail.

Occasionally, by total happenstance, Max would take a leak during one of these hours, and we would all dance around like we were at a Grateful Dead concert and they just started playing "Truckin'." "Yaaaay!" we would yell. "Max peed in the potty!" We would break open piñatas, and bring in mariachi bands, and declare amnesty for all overdue library books, and Max would laugh, and we'd say, we did it!

But we didn't do it. Weeks go by, and every day we spend a couple half-hours on the potty, and sometimes Max uses it, and sometimes he doesn't, and we go on changing eight thousand more diapers, and you notice that sometimes you're taking off one dry one and putting on another, and then, one day in the kitchen, you have this conversation:

"Honey, when was the last time you changed a wet diaper?"

"I don't mark these things on the calendar. I think it was the same night that we had sex without falling asleep in the middle."

"That long ago?"

"How about you?"

"I would like to have sex without falling asleep."

"No, how long since you changed a wet diaper?"

(This, by the way, no longer seems strange to parents. You can talk about sex and diapers in the same conversation without feeling ridiculous, which is quite sad, but also quite liberating. Losing one's pride, like losing one's hair, is hard at first, but after a while you just accept it and move on. Buddha says we must lose our pride to gain our freedom. But what does he know. He's bald too.)

So, guess what, everybody. Max seems to have potty-trained himself, when we weren't paying attention.

Sometimes, the big milestones just pass, like the roadside attraction that you missed because a good song was on the radio. Nothing to do but wave it goodbye, keep driving, and see what's around the next bend.

I tried not to pay too much attention to the Milestone Charts. We were having too much fun, now, anyway— because the videos were back! Now that Max was talking, we'd been given clearance from the Speech Therapy Nazis to slowly re-introduce television.

Thank God.

Suddenly, Dora was *back!* In our *house!* With her God-damn singing *Map!* And I *loved* it! The Wiggles were back, too, and our dance parties commenced again (although that Henry the Octopus was still freaking me out).

But as the videos returned, I started noticing a disturbing trend in what we were watching.

It started innocently enough. Max walked up to me one afternoon in the kitchen, and—out of the blue—uttered the words every father waits and waits for.

"I love you," Max said.

Oh. My. God. Max said he loves me! Oh, my heart soars! My soul sings! My teeth get whiter!

"You love me," he continued.

"Yes, Max," I stammered, not able to find the words to—

But then Max continued, in a sing-song voice, an unmistakable verse. . . .

No. Say it ain't so.

It's so.

There was no mistaking it.

The first time Max told me he loved me, and it was just him singing—

THE BARNEY THEME SONG!

How did that get into his little head? I had specifically banished Barney from our home. I'd given very careful instructions to wives and babysitters not to allow that damned purple dinosaur anywhere near my precious child.

But clearly, there is no avoiding Barney.

Or Dora, for that matter. Or JoJo, from *JoJo's Circus*, who on every episode learns some wonderful lesson—it's good to share your toys, it's good to brush your teeth, it's good to clean your room.

How awful!

Without realizing it, I'd allowed my son's television world—the precious, delightful world I believe that I actually grew up in—to be populated by . . . educational videos!

Oh, the horror.

But it was even worse.

I looked at the movies on the shelf under the TV. I'd allowed my wife to bring, from the basement, all the old videos she'd shown to Anna as a child. And I couldn't believe my eyes.

Lady and the Tramp—Disney! *101 Dalmatians*—Disney! *Bambi, Dumbo, Sleeping Beauty*—Disney! Disney! Disney!

So, let's get this straight, right now.

I hate Disney.

My hatred was cemented, of course, in the sixties, when Walt Disney decreed that no long-hairs would be admitted to Disneyland, but it started way before that. Growing up, even before I knew why, I sensed that I was a Warner Brothers kid, not a Disney kid. The gang that populated Warner Brothers cartoons—Bugs Bunny, Daffy Duck, Yosemite Sam—were tough-talking, wise-cracking, New York. Disney characters were mealy-mouthed, moralistic, Midwest. Warner was Jewish; Disney was goyish. Warner was hip; Disney was as straight as the turret on Cinderella's castle. Warner was about getting one over on the system; Disney was about the system prevailing.

Warner was chaos.

Disney was order.

I hated Disney.

To me, Disney was a world where good and evil meet, and good always prevailed, and where's the fun in that? Warner was a world where order and chaos meet, and chaos ruled. Where everybody talked in Brooklyn accents, smattering their speech with Jewish phrases (Bugs: "I don't play poker. Pinochle, and a occasionally a little pisha-paysha"), a rough-and-tumble world where tough guys wanted to rule the streets but funny guys could get by, like the neighborhood where I grew up.

How a Warner kid like me turned into a control-freak adult is a topic to ponder for another time, but I knew this was what I wanted for my son: Not a world where fathers smoke pipes by Christmas trees and good children part their hair on the side, but a world where Daffiness springs from every corner, and you keep your wits about you and laugh your way through. My son wouldn't be a wide-eyed innocent like Mickey, but a carrot-munching wise-guy like Bugs.

I banished the Disney collection to the basement, and went out and got the complete Looney Tunes collection, and sat Max down in front of the widescreen, and waited for the magic.

The first cartoon involved Bugs continually pounding Pete Puma in the head with a hammer ("How many lumps?" "Oh, three or four . . . "). In the next, Yosemite Sam kept shooting at Bugs with two six-guns. Scene after scene, my funny childhood friends are choking each other, bashing each other with sticks, stones, and baseball bats, kicking each other in the butt, tossing each other through plate-glass windows, luring each other to jump off a thousand-foot tower into a damp sponge. Don't like Bugs playing his banjo? Smash it! Don't like someone smashing your banjo? Drop an anvil on his head!

Oh, damn.

I forgot.

There was a reason cartoons went all educational on us.

It's the ones we grew up with.

They are astoundingly, unrelentingly, violent.

I popped from cartoon to cartoon, hoping that I'd just hit a bad batch, but it turns out: Every punchline in every Warner Brothers cartoon, somebody's getting punched. Even in the Bugs Bunny version of "Goldilocks and the Three Bears," the main joke is that whatever Baby Bear says, Daddy Bear whacks him one across the mouth.

Here's Max, at an age where a successful playdate is one in which nobody bites anyone, and here's his dad, showering him with images demonstrating just how funny it is to stick somebody's finger in an electric socket (fairly funny, but not as hysterical as handing someone a lit firecracker, tying a noose around their neck and yanking really hard, or that old standby, hitting them in the face with a shovel and watching them vibrate like a tuning fork).

My attempts to teach Max how humor can triumph over pretension was lost in a blizzard of bullets, bombs, and blackjacks.

What an ultra-maroon.

Reluctantly, we returned to *Dora the Explorer.* ("Daddy showed you violent cartoons because he's an *IDIOT!* Can you say *IDIOT?* In Spanish, we say *IDIOTA!* Can you say *IDIOTA?"*)

As Max rounded the far turn of two-and-a-half, the Milestone Charts were particularly crazy-making. They told us that at this age most kids can wash and dry their hands (Max could turn on the water, fill a cup, and empty it on the floor, does that count?), balance on one foot (hey! We got that one!), speak clearly all the time (well, not that one) and name one friend.

Friend?

He's supposed to have friends?

Oh, shit! We forgot to find other kids!

Somehow, for older parents, it's easy to make that mistake. Most of the parents our age were sending kids off to college, and most of the parents of kids Max's age were not so far out of college themselves—they lived in urban areas or suburban cul-de-sacs with other folks their age, who had kids their kids' ages. These young parents had friends who were getting to be parents around the same time. Our friends were sending their kids to the prom, not to the playground. So we had plenty of teenagers around for babysitting duty, and for $12 an hour we had plenty of freedom. We were the only parents of a toddler who won the Oscar pool because we'd seen all the movies.

But friends?

God damn. How much do they charge an hour for those?

Turns out, they're hard to rent.

Turns out, you have to take out a long-term lease.

They call it preschool.

When you enter the world of preschools in any urban setting, you're immediately confronted with all sorts of questions about what sort of parent you are. And if you're not careful, you can get sucked into the Vortex of Shame.

One minute, you're sitting in a tiny chair in a room painted in primary colors, waiting your turn to talk to the nice lady who runs a preschool with an annoyingly cute name—there's the Little Learners, Learn-and-Play, Play-and-Learn, Learn-Play-Then-Learn-Some-More, Play-Play-Play-Learn-Play-Learn, and so on (unless, of course, you step over into the world of religious affiliation, in which case you've got Saint Mary Ignatius Dayschool, Shlomo Raven Preschool, or, for the ecumenical, Saint Moshe's Play-and-Learn)—and you're sitting patiently, idly passing the time by working the Play-Doh spaghetti maker, and the next minute you're hearing the parent ahead of you discussing the curriculum (curriculum?!) and expectations (expectations??) and whether their little Kristin will be challenged (challenged!!) enough by a non-Montessori structure because ever since she began counting past 100 it's been difficult to find an environment that's stimulating enough (Stimulating? I've spent the last two years trying to keep Max quiet for 10 minutes a day. I was supposed to be stimulating him? I've got a book pile from the top of which I can see Canada—why didn't one of them tell me I was supposed to be stimulating!).

—and suddenly, you realize that Max is not just a loving, laughing, emerging consciousness. He's a student, and you are the teacher, and you forgot to create a syllabus, or come to class, and now he's terribly behind, and he'll never catch up, or go to a good college, and he'll wind up in a job where he has to wear a paper hat.

You try to resist this, these yuppie notions of competitive parenting—and by the way, did you know that the term was originally "Yappies"? It was a play on "Yippies." The yippies—both an acronym for the Youth International Party, and itself a play on the word "hippies"—were led by Abbie Hoffman and Jerry Rubin, and represented one of the many vain attempts to leverage the great emotional strength of the Woodstock Generation into an ongoing political tool—and boy, we must have been really stoned to think we were going to accomplish that! I did one of the last in-depth interviews with Abbie Hoffman. The last time I talked to him, in early 1989, he was talking about starting, of all things, a sports handicapping business; he was looking for an advertising firm, and I suggested a few, but he rejected them because they were too big. He liked to work with the little guys. He was calling collect from an airport, where he was about to board a plane to go give a lecture to college students about keeping hope alive. A few days later, he was found in his bed in his home, a converted turkey coop near, appropriately, New Hope, Pennsylvania. The coroner found the remains of 150 phenobarbitol pills in his stomach, and ruled the death a suicide. He left three children, then aged 28, 26, and 17, and "not a yuppie in the litter," he had told me proudly. He was the genuine article.

Anyway, by around 1983, the term "yappies" started to appear, as people struggled to define the baby-boomer generation—YAP, for young, aspiring professionals. The term didn't stick, probably because it recalled the somewhat anti-Semitic (not to mention anti-Asian) term "Jap," for Jewish American Princess, which appeared around the same time—but it stuck around long enough to spawn *Y.A.P.: The Official Young Aspiring Professional's Fast Track Handbook* that summer. By 1984, the term had morphed into "Yumpies," for young upwardly mobile professionals. But that didn't stick either, because, to tell the truth, we weren't all that upwardly mobile. Our parents owned their own homes; because of inflation, recession, and being too stoned, most of us could barely afford our own cars. But we were working on it, and by the middle of that year the term "yuppies"—young urban professionals—had taken a firm hold, as did the lifestyle that went along with it, which included, unfortunately, the swilling of expensive if sour white wines, the purchasing of condos, and the onslaught of competitive parenting.

Now, 20 years later, I'm sitting in some WASPy lady's basement, listening to these parents discuss whether the pre-primary school would interfere with their kids' Suzuki lessons (and not daring to ask—are they talking about the violin, or is their kid already driving a motorcycle?), and I'm trying not to get sucked into the Vortex of Shame, because of what a bad parent I am. But it's too late.

Morose, I drive from one WASPy lady's basement to the next, knowing Max is already too far behind to ever catch up, that he will be the three-year-old equivalent of Gomer Pyle (loved for his goofiness and uncanny ability to drop his silly accent when it comes time to sing, but never called on to break the secret codes)—when, thank my lucky stars, I tripped across Kenwood Learn and Play, which we soon came to know as Miss Diane's School.

Miss Diane was the antidote for all those yuppie fears. The Kenwood Learn and Play consisted of her basement, which included a couch, some blocks, some cars, a table, some crayons, a yard with some more cars, and about seven kids bouncing on the couch. Her school philosophy seemed to be: If the kids get through the day without hurting themselves too badly, and I get through without going crazy, we'll call it a success.

I loved Miss Diane.

Max's entrance test seemed to consist of seeing whether he would say "Hello Miss Diane," which he did, and whether he would play with the other children, which he didn't, because he apparently had never seen other children before. So of those two questions, he got one right. Fortunately, the passing grade on this exam was 50 percent, so we were in! Max would actually get to interact with other human beings his own age, three mornings a week!

Now there was only one problem left.

Getting myself to let him go.

The night before my great big two-and-a-half-year-old man started Miss Diane's School, I couldn't sleep. I was still awake at 3 a.m., when Max, as he had begun doing, started intoning, "*Mama* love baby . . . mama love baby. . . ." It was like a mantra he used, to make her appear. I went into his room, and lay down with him, and he looked at me, and said, "Mama love baby." Clearly, the magic wasn't working right. Daddy appeared. How do you adjust this thing?

More and more, I started to become jealous of Rachel. Max had taken to randomly announcing, "No want da-da! Want mommy!" How could she have this spell over this child? Why can't I have that spell? What's so bad about daddies? We are much funnier than mommies! We can carry you farther! We are the ones who will teach you to drive! If we ever let you have the keys, that is. But still!

I lay down next to Max, who was cuddling with his latest love object, the big soft yellow Moon with the smiling face, named, of course, Mister Moon.

"Dada love baby," I offered.

"Dada love baby," Max replied. Yes! But then . . .

"Baby love Mister Moon," he continued. "Night night Mister Moon. Baby love mama. Mama love baby." It was like cuddling with the Magic Eight Ball, knowing the words that float to the surface are random, but secretly believing they hold the truth about your future. "Night night Mister Moon," he said, and drifted off to sleep.

"Baby love dada?" I tried, knowing he was asleep, and knowing what the Magic Eight Ball always said when you asked the good stuff:

Ask Again Later.

The next morning the alarm went through me like a knife. It's time! I bolted out of bed like Ricky when he thought Lucy was having the baby. If I wore a fedora, I'd have slept in it. It's time! It's time! Max is . . . leaving home!

Here's the thing of it, guys. The cliché about us is that we don't know how to relate to kids until they're about four, when they can get jokes, when they can catch the ball, when they can wrestle, when they can help us wash the car, when they can go to the fridge and bring back a beer (admit it, that is about as cool as it gets, right? Your friends love that, right? Even if you don't drink beer, you put beers in the fridge so the kid can go get you one in front of your friends. It's like the first time you had a girlfriend who did laundry— no one can believe what a lucky little fucker you are.).

But the truth of it is, guys need babies more than mothers do.

We have, because we are The Most Important Gender On the Planet, been very busy, what with building all the roads and bridges and writing *Lolita* and *For Whom the Bell Tolls* and figuring out nuclear fission and all. Granted, each of us didn't participate in all of that, but hey, there's no "I" in team. It doesn't matter which of us actually figured out how to produce the Oreo cookie, the greatest food known to hu-mankind, and which of us figured out exactly how long you should dunk it in the milk; the point is, it was the Boys' Camp that got all that done.

And as a result of being so Important and Busy, we lost touch with what I was beginning to understand was the Tao of Max. Some believe "the peace that passes under-standing" comes only from Christ; others use the term for the state of grace achieved only by meditation; for me, and for most dads, it is the feeling that comes from having a child who is too young to speak, or walk, or do just about anything, and who brings you to a state of equilibrium when no one's in the house but you and him, and his dia-pers are clean and he is bathed and fed and not yet ready to sleep, and you just. . . . Sit.

And you put on the "New Morning" CD again, and Bob Dylan sings:

Ain't no reason to go in the wagon to town
Ain't no reason to go to the fair
Ain't no reason to go up, ain't no reason to go down
Ain't no reason to go . . . anywhere.

And in that pause, the inhalation before he sings "any-where," in that tiny moment of silence and solitude, you in-hale as well, and sit, and you are separated for a moment from the camp of achievers, you and your son. And that, when he was a baby, was the Tao of Max: Ain't no reason to go . . . anywhere.

And that is why men need babies.

And that is why I was so sad on this morning.

Because Max was taking a big step, not a baby step.

And I was about to, quite literally, Send Him Packing.

Because Max was in such a mommy phase, we decided that I would be the one to take him to school on his first day, since separating from me would be easier than separating from mommy, although I would have cut off a pinkie for that not to be the case. There was a very tearful moment at the door as he left the house (mommy's tears, not Max's); with the fire-engine backpack on his back about as big as he was, he seemed like a little turtle headed off from home—self-protected and self-sufficient. As we drove to school, I made up a little song to keep him cheerful:

We're gonna play with trucks today,
Trucks today, trucks today,
We're gonna play with trucks today,
At Miss Diane's School.
We're going to school-to-day,
We're gonna play-and-play,
We're gonna play-all-day,
At Miss Diane's School-to-daaaaaay.

Max thought this was very funny. "Again!" he ordered. And "Again!"—joining in on a few words here and there.

It's amazing how quickly your own brilliant creativity turns mawkish and sour and painful once you've had to perform it four or five hundred times. This is why Mike Nesmith quit the Monkees.

By the time we approached Miss Diane's School, where I was blissfully delivered from having to sing the Miss Diane's School song any more, I realized that the song had not been there to distract Max from his fears, but to distract me from mine. Holy shit! I am for the first time about to leave Max in a Strange Place with Strangers who will do Strange Things (strange in that they Do Not Involve Me)! As we walked down the driveway, and stopped to pat the little statuary of a hedgehog on its head, it occurred to me: Why do Gentiles love to have little statues of woodland animals on their lawns? This is not a Jewish thing. Maybe it's a leftover from the days that we weren't supposed to be making craven images and false idols while Moses was up on the mountain having a bowl of borscht with God, and he came down and saw the big golden calf—which, how dumb could the Jews have been anyway, God or no God, to take all the gold and melt it down and form it into a calf? Who does this? Don't you have anything better to do with your time? Get a job!— or maybe hedgehogs are in and of themselves not Jewish, because what Jew knows from woodland creatures anyway? There were no hedgehogs in the Bronx. See, another reason you know that Disney is Gentile and Warner Brothers are Jewish. Chip and Dale. Who the hell knew from chipmunks? Tweety birds in a cage in the apartment window, chased by a hungry alley cat, OK. Even Foghorn Leghorn, while technically a barnyard animal, was a takeoff on Senator Cleghorn, a character on the radio show of Fred Allen, who, while as an Irish Catholic was technically not Jewish, seemed Jewish, because he had characters in "Allen's Alley" with thick Jewish accents, and because his writers were Jewish, and because my Grandma Fagel (remember her? The one who looks like George Washington?) proclaimed that he was Jewish, as she did with any performer she liked. "See der Greta Garbo?" she would say. "I tink is really Greta Garfinkle."

So now we are at the door of Miss Diane's, and I cannot breathe, and I wonder what strange rituals they will perform here—what are those fingerpaints for? Those blocks? Will they build crosses and paint stigmata on their palms? What have I done?—And Max runs in, and drops his backpack, and Miss Diane instructs him to place it on a hook—already, rules rules rules! I have delivered my son to a military camp!—and he gladly does, and runs to the corner where he has spotted some cars to play with—and there are two other children, two incredibly blond, blue-eyed children—what are they going to have for snack, ham with mayonnaise on white bread?—oh, no wait, there in the kitchen area are the Ritz crackers and Kraft American cheese and Juicy Juice boxes, familiar touchstones in this strange world, but still, I cannot breathe, I cannot move, and the kindly Miss Diane has made sure Max is settled in, and puts a hand on my shoulder, and says, I think it's time for Daddy to say good-bye, and my heart jumps out of my body and lies on the floor, where the blond blue-eyes start jumping up and down on it, and with my soulless lifeless zombie form floating through this netherworld of its own accord I kneel down next to Max, summoning all my strength to console him for the painful separation tantrum that I know is inevitable, and I tell him to give me a hug goodbye.

"Dis a red truck da-da! I find a red truck!"

What a brave trouper. I gather him in my arms, and bury my face in his impossibly perfect hair, and whisper, "Daddy loves you. Mommy will pick you up in a little while."

And I look up, ready for the torrent of tears. And Max, beautiful child that he is, finds the words to express his feelings in this moment.

"Bye Da-da! Dis a fire truck! I find a fire truck! Woo woo woo woo wooo!"

So brave. How has he learned to hide his fear so well? Have I taught him to suppress his feelings? Is that a bad thing?

"Bye bye, Da-da," I hear. "Maxie loves his daddy. He'll see you very soon."

My God, those reassuring words! Where did Max learn . . . oh, no, it was Miss Diane, trying to usher me out the door.

On the way back up the driveway, I patted the hedge-hog one more time for luck, got in my car, and drove away. There were so many more tears than I had expected.

Mine, of course. Not Max's.

Max was to be at Miss Diane's School for three hours. Rachel decided that, just in case he was having troubles, she'd show up to pick him up a little early.

Like, three hours early. She passed me in the driveway, in front of the disapproving gaze of the hedgehog.

Actually, she was a little later than that, but not much. She called me at work to say she was sitting in her car, and watching Max in Miss Diane's backyard, and he seemed to be doing fine. I told her to go to a Starbucks or something, because we didn't want to seem like the kind of neurotic parents who spy on their kids at school. Of course, that is exactly what kind of neurotic parents we are. We just didn't want to seem like it.

That night, as I put him to bed, Max seemed so much older. It seemed like he had returned from a far-away trip. I checked his backpack to see if there were the stickers on it you see on the trunks in old movies—Bombay, Hong Kong, Chattanooga—and was almost surprised to see they weren't there. Through that fall and winter, I struggled to deal with the strangest feeling of all: My son was beginning to have a life separate from mine. So was our teen-ager: She would actually leave the house with friends on a weekend morning, and not come home until after dinner, and I would marvel at the fact that she was living her life so separate from us, and then I would look at Max, and realize that he, in his way, was doing the same, and that it would always be thus, and all I could do was hang on to what I could hang on to, and learn to let go of the rest.

As Max's third birthday approached, we decided there was one matter on which we could not use the Foolproof Parenting System ("Just wait, it will change"). Max, the doctor told us, was developing Pacifier Gap. This, it turns out, is not the name of a town in the old west, but a pushing forward of the top teeth caused by overuse of the nookie.

Actually, we never used a cute name like "nookie" for the pacifier (and what sicko decided to use the same nickname for pacifiers and sex anyway? Not that they're not both quite calming, but really. That's over the line. Although it does give me great pleasure to hang out in Buy Buy Baby and listen to the suburban housewives asking the clerks, "Where is the nookie section?" Hey, you take your vicarious thrills where you find them. I find them in the nookie section).

So Max and I agreed that when his third birthday came, we would pack up all the pacifiers and mail them to the Babies Who Don't Have Pacifiers. We had a little birthday party for him, and afterward we gathered up all the pacifiers and put them in a box, and stamped it, and daddy took it out to the "post office" (actually the garage, but please don't tell Max), and that night, we lay down in bed, and I told Max how proud I was of him.

"Thank you Daddy."

"You're welcome, Max."

"Daddy?"

"Yes, my darling."

"I want a pacifier."

When I reminded him that we had mailed them away, he gave me a look of utter shock and disgust. You mean, that wasn't a game? You were doing that FOR REAL?

—and he started wailing like I've never heard him before. You know the song, "Turn Back the Hands of Time"? Not the soppy violin-soaked ballad R. Kelly did, where he tries to turn into Sam Cooke at the end, or that ridiculous pop song of the same title that Eddie Fisher did way back when. I mean, of course, the great old-school song version by Tyrone Davis, who sang not one but two of the best songs of regret: his version of "Can I Change My Mind" is the song he's better remembered for now (with the one-line chorus, "I would like to, Start all over again"), but at the time, his bigger hit was "Turn Back the Hands of Time"—it was incredible, as was "Change My Mind," for playing a light, almost danceable tune against searingly painful lyrics ("Oh the pain's so deep, the hurting's getting stronger. . . . ")

There I was, in bed with Tyrone Davis, his pain so deep without his pacifier, pleading with me to turn back the hands of time.

"I not three, I two," he wailed. "I a baby. I need pacifiers. Daddy, go get them. I crying." ("I'm so lonely without you," Tyrone sang, "Can't sleep at night always think about you.")

I cuddled Tyrone in my arms, and told him the story of our two favorite cats, Fee-Fee and Foo-Foo, whom I had created a few months earlier; their little rhyming escapades had taken us on great adventures ("Fee-Fee and Foo-Foo were two little cats, who went 'round the world, imagine that! They first went to Italy, where pasta they mangia; then down to Jamaica, to buy up some ganja"). On this night, the two cats flew to the land of babies who cried because they did not have pacifiers, and Fee-Fee and Foo-Foo, who were now three years old, didn't need them anymore, so they gave the pacifiers to the babies. And Max stopped crying, and listened, lulled by the gentle rhythms and lapping rhymes, and his eyes got heavy, and he cuddled against me, and when it was all over, he looked up at me, love and hope in his eyes, and said: "I need pacifiers. Daddy gets them."

OK, so sometimes dads can't do everything.

In fact, sometimes they can't do anything.

I don't know how Max got to sleep that night, or the next, but I do know that by day three, his personality was gone. He was cranky and irritable and rotten, and—well, exactly like I was, when I quit smoking. It was like having a methadone addict in the house—he was off the heroin, but the alternative seemed much worse.

On the third night, he started talking a blue streak, like he'd never talked before. About ants, which we saw in the kitchen. Itchies—he had itchies. About the song he calls "A-Adorable," the song my father sang me, which I had started singing to Max, which he would not allow me to sing since we took the pacifiers away. He was going on and on: talking about underwear and airplanes and tummy aches, and how mommy is downstairs making lots of noise with an orange vacuum cleaner—it was as though by taking away the pacifier we had unplugged him, and all the words were pouring out.

But at the end of his dissertation he came to his conclusion: I am Max. Max needs pacifiers. Therefore I need pacifiers. How hard is that to understand? When he realized that they were not forthcoming, he started crying again, and I started to worry that he was going to make himself sick.

And he did.

Max woke up the next morning with a 103-degree temperature, drooping and dripping with sweat. He just curled up on the couch, not even wanting to watch TV, which was a really bad sign. I dragged myself off to work, miserable. I didn't really think the cold and the pacifier were linked, but I knew how much it would help him through this day.

I made a fatherly decision.

"Rachel," I said into the phone, "I've decided we should let him have the pacifier back."

"Good," she said. "I already did."

It's not giving up control that is hardest for men, when they become dads. It's giving up the illusion of control. That's the tricky part.

And, as far as the addiction to pacifiers went, we made the decision to go back to the brilliant, time-tested parenting philosophy:

Just wait. It will change.

Happy birthday, Max. Three years old. How could that be? We've been doing this thing together for more than a thousand days. You don't even know the number a thousand. We've only counted to twenty. But trust me, that's a long, long time. Forty and a half inches, 34 pounds, three years old. My goodness. You are such a big boy. Last week, we watched our first movie together, a whole movie, all the way through, just you and daddy. It was Yellow Submarine. You loved it, and have watched it over and over. The other night, I was putting you to bed, and I sang that bouncy little one-two-three-four number, "All Together Now," and you interrupted and said, "Daddy who sing dat?" and, not thinking, I told you, "John sings that." And you corrected me! "No, Daddy, John no sing dat. John sing 'All You Need Is Love.'"

Curious, I sang a few lines from "Only a Northern Song"—you love the psychedelic scene in the movie that has that song in it—and I asked you who sang it. "Dat George, Daddy." "And, um Max, who sings 'Yellow Submarine'?" "Dat Ringo, Daddy. He play drums."

My genius.

It's just like the song I sing to you by John Sebastian, my darling: I have waited, since you toddled, for the great relief of having you to talk to.

This is you and me, now, on our way to Miss Diane's School: I sing the first line of "When I'm Sixty-Four," and you sing the part that goes: "Doo-do-DOO-do-do!" Right on the beat, too.

You are too much, my son. And soon, we will have all the time in the world to sing. I know you like to go to Daddy's office, and play with the toys on my shelf. But Daddy told his boss that he's going to stop working there, very soon. Daddy's gonna work at home now, in his office upstairs, so we can have more time together. I hope you're going to like that. I know I am.

You know, I thought of another Daddy song. It was by a group called Shep and the Limelites. This guy Shep was in another band, and they did a song called "You're A Thousand Miles Away." It was very pretty. When Shep joined the Limelites, he used the same tune for a song called "Daddy's Home." It means a lot to me, right now. It's about a father who finds out his child is crying, and he promises to come home and never leave the child alone again.

You are crying, right now, because of this pacifier thing we're going through, and I'm so, so sorry. But soon, my Max, we will have all the time in the world, time to dry your tears, time to sing together, time for so many other things. All the time in the world, which is the greatest gift I can imagine. Because, get ready, my boy: I'm not a thousand miles away, anymore. Daddy's home.

7

Finding Dadditude

Way back at the beginning of this book—and have I mentioned lately that I think it's really damn nice of you to have stayed with me so long? I don't think authors thank their readers enough. Really, when you think about it, they should be kissing your damned feet, them going on for hundreds of pages about whatever the hell it is, war, peace, whether Jesus had a kid with Mary Magdalene, bla bla bla, and expecting you to keep paying attention, when really it's just that you probably shelled out a couple of sawbucks for the thing and you don't want to look like a putz paying for books you didn't read, so on you slog. Look at this book so far. What are we, 169 pages in, and the kid just turned three years old? I can hear you saying, get on with it! And on with it I shall get—but I do have to retrace my steps for a moment, because way back in the beginning, when I said that all three-year-olds are basically lunatics, I was not being fair, at all.

To be fair, I should have been more specific about the term "lunatic."

Ancient psychologists, meaning, anyone who came before Dr. Phil, used to think that lunacy was caused by the
moon—hence, the root "luna," and the official designation
of the American College of Psychiatrists and Other Bearded
People for those suffering from mental disorders: "He's totally looney-tunes."

To this day, most police persons, I must tell you from my
experience of working with them for 15 years, still believe
that aberrant behavior is connected to the full moon. It
doesn't matter how much crime happens during the other 27
days of the lunar cycle: on the night of the full moon, every
cop treats every crime as though it were werewolf-related.
All our hotline operators at *America's Most Wanted* believed
it too: "Guy called up last night and said the government is
controlling his mind through the fillings in his teeth," they
would say, tossing the tip sheet on my desk, and adding
with a knowing look: "Full moon last night." As though the
day before that, he did not suffer from this delusion, instead
being fully cognizant of the truth, which is that the government is not controlling his mind through the fillings in his
teeth, but rather through the transmitter they installed when
he thought he was having his tonsils removed.

But modern psychologists understand that the moon has
little, if anything, to do with most personality disorders.
Which is too bad, because then there would be the hope
that with the exception of one night of the month, your
three-year-old might act like a normal human being.

Instead—and again, I apologize for having used the
vague term "lunatic," which I will now correct—they suffer,
for approximately one year, from a rare affliction known as
"pan-disorder."

That is: they have every mental illness that exists on the market today, as well as a few that are still in the beta-testing stage.

Now you may be saying, "Phil, if I may call you Phil, and by the way that is a very attractive picture of you on the back flap of the book, how can you say every child suffers from every mental disorder? Don't you think you're being a bit harsh and oversimplistic?"

To which I would reply, why of course. If you haven't noticed yet, that's my job.

Nevertheless, to be fair, I will note that there are a few documented cases of three-year-old children in Idaho and Ohio who were suspected not to be out of their minds; and one toddler in Worcester, Massachusetts, who was said to be downright sane. Scientists are still examining these claims.

But for the rest of us, here are just some of the disorders of which Max showed all the symptoms, right after he turned three:

Multiple personality disorder: "Max, have some more peas." "No! I hate peas! Yuck! I allergic to peas! Peas make me sick!" "Max, you were eating them five minutes ago. You finished a whole bowl and asked for more." "Dat not me! Someone else eat da peas! I no eat dem! Waaaaah!"

Manic depression: It is late morning. Max is lying on the couch, staring at the television, which his mom left on earlier when she was watching *The Today Show*. Now, that channel is showing *The Price Is Right*. Max knows how to use the remote, and can even find the cartoon channels, but at the moment does not have the energy. He is splayed out on the couch, watching a very excited woman make the painfully crucial decision about whether a large bottle of Advil or a pair of green flip-flops is more likely to cost $6.95, as a man who looks like Bob Barker, if he were 179 years old—wait, that is Bob Barker, he is 179 years old—is hovering nearby. How could Bob possibly still need to do this? Jeez, he's been doing price-comparisons for all these years, he couldn't have blown all his dough. What happens when he goes to the supermarket? "I'll just take these five oranges." "That'll be one million dollars, Mister Barker." "Oh, my, that seems like a lot. Guess I'll have to do the show for two more years."

Max cannot possibly understand the concept of trying to decide the prices of these objects—no matter what I bring home, Max announces, "that cost you forty-seven cents"—but he is suffering from such malaise and ennui that he cannot muster the energy to press the button on the remote, which is resting on his tummy. I suggest that we turn off the TV and go to the pool. He does not have the energy to respond, not even the "uuungh" that I can sometimes get out of his teenaged sister in the same moment of repose. So I turn off the television, at which point I hear a noise that convinces me that a jet plane has crashed into the roof. "NOOOO!" Max screams. "Me want to turn it off! NOOOOOO!" Screaming, rending of garments, gnashing of teeth, tossing of plates. I quickly relent, turning the TV back on and allowing Max to turn it off.

This activity seems to please him no end, because he is now bouncing up and down, racing from the kitchen to the dining room and back, shouting, "Me turn off! Me turn off!

Me turn off!" I try to channel this energy into getting ready to go to the pool, which feels like the equivalent of putting a tuxedo on a jackhammer. "Go to pool! Go to pool! Waaa-hoooo!" Max is wailing. A sandal goes on, a bathing suit goes on, a sandal comes off; a T-shirt goes on, a bathing suit comes off. He is laughing hysterically. The more frustrated I get, the funnier he thinks it is.

"Max, please stop wiggling."

"Wiggle! Wiggle! Wiggle! Wiggle! Wiggle!"

"Max, if you do not stop, we will not go to the pool."

"Wiggle! Wiggle! Wiggle! Wiggle! Wiggle!"

"Max, was there a full moon last night?"

"Wiggle! Wiggle! Wiggle! Wiggle! Wiggle!"

Finally, somehow, I get Max into his swimsuit and hat, and look despondently at the sunscreen—I know putting this on him is going to be like trying to baste the Thanksgiving turkey while it's still alive, but I persevere, remembering the cardinal rule: do not grease any part of him you may have to hold on to while you're greasing the other parts. Astoundingly, I manage to lube the boy, and repeat the process with the bug spray. Now it is time to try to pack the beach bag with only the essentials—more sunscreen, more bug spray, a ball, some cars, three towels, dry clothes, an extra bathing suit, some cheese, a Go-GURT yogurt, some pretzels, an apple, Max's sunglasses, my sunglasses, my reading glasses, *The New York Times* (like yeah, right, that's totally gonna happen), a big ball, a little ball, the floaty-arm-thingies, Mister Duck, Momma Duck, and a box of raisins. All the while, Daffy Duck is bouncing off the walls, tossing things out of the beach bag as fast as I can put them in, shouting, "Towel fly! Bug spray fly! Annuda towel fly!" and now I cannot grab him and stop him, because he is so slippery from the sunscreen he could probably slide all the way to the pool—but exhausted and triumphant, somehow, I have the beach bag re-packed, and I run upstairs and change into my bathing suit in 7.3 seconds—if only there were Olympics for the events dads have to be good at, we'd really kick some international butt—and I come downstairs, and call out, in my happiest voice, "OK, buddy, time for the pool!"

And there is Max, splayed out on the couch, motionless and emotionless, staring vaguely at the tube, as a woman ponders the deep spiritual question of whether a half-dozen Sharpies of varied colors could possibly sell for less than two purple quart bottles of Palmolive Dish Soap with Aloe, as Bob Barker tries to simulate a facial expression indicating that he is still alive.

"Max," I say, my voice trembling in fear, "Don't you still want to go to the pool?"

He does not move, he does not look up.

"Max, really, time to go! Hey hey hey!"

He musters all the energy he has to take a deep breath, and in a tone as devoid of energy as Bob Barker's libido itself, he utters: "Uuuuuhngh."

Manic depression takes many forms. Few are as clear as this. Oddly, true manic depressives only change moods a few times a day, if that; Max can oscillate from delirium to enervation like a metronome.

Attention-deficit hyperactivity disorder: Please. This goes without saying.

Alzheimer's disease: I know, they say this disorder, characterized by loss of memory, is found only in senior citizens. Not so. To wit:

"Max, take your plate to the sink."

"OK, Daddy!"

Max leaves his plate and walks toward the playroom.

"Max, what did Daddy just say?"

"Um, play ball?"

Munchausen syndrome: Named for Baron Von Munchausen, who was not nearly as exciting as the stories about him, this is a disorder in which a patient feigns symptoms of illness in order to get attention or a desired treatment—or, as any parent knows, "I too sick to go to school." "Max, it's Saturday, there's no school." "I recover miraculously, it baffles science!"

Tourette's syndrome: This also goes without saying. You doodyhead.

Exhibitionism: This seems to be a particular favorite of three-year-old girls, who seem to talk best while pulling their dresses over their heads, but Max shows many symptoms—mainly, when I'm changing him, especially in a public place, like the beach, as soon as I get his clothes off, he takes off running. There is really nothing wrong with this, and there is nothing so liberating and delightful and soothing to the soul as a little naked three-year-old running on the beach, and I try to allow myself to revel in this perfect moment, but I, myself, remain in shock, years after the fact, from a failed experiment we called Naked Hour.

It was when Max was almost two. We were alone in the house, and I had just given him a bath, and decided not to get him dressed right away. I was soaking wet myself, as I always was after the splashfest of a bath—people jump off diving boards with their clothes on and stay dryer than a parent who has just bathed a two-year-old—and I thought, what ever happened to the old hippie in me? When did I get so uptight? We need some naked time around this house! So, a little more trepidatiously than I'm really comfortable admitting, and since my stepdaughter was away at her dads and free from any possible trauma, I declared Naked Hour. Max and I read a book, and played with a car, and lounged around, in the buff, and it was really quite lovely, until he ran out of the room, and I started after him, and noticed, on the carpet . . . a small brown footprint.

Alarmed, I looked toward the door, and sure enough: a series of small brown footprints, all headed in the direction of my hysterically laughing son, who is headed in the direction of the not-so-hysterically expensive rug in the dining room.

Dear reader, I will take this moment to remind you that Naked Hour is not a great idea until well after children are potty-trained.

Desperately dragging my poop-footed son back to the bath, I pondered the task ahead of me—somehow scrub down the rugs, the carpets, the walls (how the hell did it get on the walls?), the dog (the dog?), while watching Max, and getting it all done before Rachel gets home and declares that the substance I have allowed Max to track all over our home is the same substance my brains are made of.

So, to this day, we now celebrate Underwear Hour instead. Max is well potty trained, by now, and as soon as I get the image of that day out of my mind, we will try Naked Hour again. My therapist is estimating that by that time, Max will be seventy-three.

Mogo on the gogo: An affliction referred to in passing in the film *Spellbound*. Two characters are talking about love. "Mogo on the gogo" has something to do with finding out that reality and fantasy are not one in the same, and being miserable as a result. This is what happened to Max when I had to explain to him why he could not have an actual playdate with SpongeBob SquarePants.

Kleptomania: This started as soon as Max entered Miss Diane's School. He came home and started playing with a car I didn't recognize. "Max, where did you get that?" I asked. "School," he said. "I borrow it." "Did Miss Diane say you could borrow it?"

Long silence.

"Max, did Miss Diane say you could borrow it?"

Longer silence.

"Max, was there a full moon last night?"

Turns out, Max had been clipping cars from Miss Diane's for about a week. Like a squirrel, he was stashing them in his playroom, next to the car wash. From that day forth, we had to pat him down whenever he left school, somebody else's house, a toy store, the supermarket, or the barber's ("I neeeeeeeed that comb, Daddy! I neeeeeeeeed it!" This, it turns out, is exactly how Al Capone got started, only with him, it wasn't cars and combs, it was machine guns. Those were *not* careful parents).

Clearly, the list could go on: Max, at various moments, showed the symptoms of acute stress disorder, insomnia, schizo-affective syndrome, dyspepsia, encopresis, folie à deux, sleepwalking, transvestism (although we didn't worry about that—he looks so cute in his sister's high heels), panic attacks, narcolepsy, hypochondria, primary neurosis, secondary neurosis, primary psychosis, secondary psychosis, agoraphobia, hydrophobia, ephebophobia, triskaidekaphobia, and the willies.

And lest you think I am singling Max out to garner sympathy, I assure you, Max was one of the easy ones. You shoulda seen the other kids in his class.

So the question is not, "Is my three-year-old a lunatic" (although he is), or even "Is my three-year-old as much of a lunatic as that other kid" (no, you can always find another kid who is worse, to make yourself feel better; this, in fact, is a primary occupation of most parents, replacing the kinds of activities that took up your energies before parenthood, like gin rummy, Italian cinema, and oral sex).

No, my friends, the question is, which of his many, many mental illnesses will come to the forefront when my child is three years old?

In the case of Max Wilder Lerman, as in the case of most three-year-olds on the planet, the answer was simple.

It was obsessive-compulsive disorder.

Obsessive-compulsives fixate on repetitive actions as a way to ward off recurring negative thoughts. In Max's case, the recurring negative thought seemed to be this:

"NOOOOOOOOOOOOOOOOOOOOOOOOOOOOO!"

This is about as negative a thought as you can get. Shortly after Max turned three, our days became largely a matter of avoiding this negative thought.

And thus were born the repetitive actions.

I remember sitting in the theater watching *As Good As It Gets,* in which Jack Nicholson plays a writer with OCD—we in the know like to refer to our diseases by their initials; it's our way of being intimate with the thing we fear the most—a writer who wouldn't step on cracks, wouldn't use the same piece of soap twice, that sort of thing. I wondered why all the parents kept smiling and whispering to each other, "Look! Just like little Johnny!" especially since their kid was named Dylan.

I do not wonder any more.

They were whispering because their kids were three years old, and the obsessive-compulsive behaviors were driving their parents crazy.

Max's obsessive behaviors began with the concept of a race. Shortly after he started walking, he started running, and shortly after he started running, he wanted to race. Racing was his favorite activity; losing, unfortunately, was his least favorite. So, not only did we have to race every-where, but I had to lose. OK, I could handle this; who hasn't let a little kid win at something (or made the HUGE mistake of trying to teach him that losing is part of life, and that you can't win 'em all: If Max ever lost a race, he would lie on the ground and scream and pound his fists on the floor. He learned this, of course, from George Steinbrenner, although when could George Steinbrenner have actually met Max? This is still a mystery to me).

No, letting Max win every race was not hard.

It was when every step I took became a race that this became difficult.

One morning, after breakfast, I was taking the dishes from the dining room to the kitchen. Max started screaming: "Wait! Wait! we race!" He ran up next to me, shouted, "Go!" and took off for the kitchen.

How adorable, I thought.

I did not think this long.

For weeks, I could not get up from bed at night to take a pee without hearing a little voice from the next room: "Wait! We race!" (How did he know?) Up the stairs, down the stairs, kitchen to pantry: I felt like some old lady who couldn't cross the street without some crazed Boy Scout insisting on helping her. Max was everywhere, and everywhere we raced.

But that was only the start.

Obsessive behaviors began to sprout up everywhere, as though he'd gotten a box of them at his third birthday party. Which in itself was a nightmare, by the way—I don't know whose idea it was to tell Max, you know, it's not like we don't indulge you enough, but there's a day coming up called your birthday, when we're really going to go overboard, and go to the party store and come back with the little race-car-motif paper plates, with matching cups and napkins and tablecloth, and the banner, and the balloons, of course, you have to have balloons, and then the party favors, and the goodie bags to go by the front door when the kids leave, with their names on them because they can all read their names now, and the noisemakers, which is ridiculous because giving a noisemaker to a three-year-old is like giving more ego to Rush Limbaugh, it's not like they need the help, and the fruit juices with cartoon characters on the box, and those annoying little straws that you can never poke through the hole, and mac and cheese with broccoli and apple slices, no, we couldn't just order a damn pizza—and we were giving what is known in parent circles as a "very small party." We'd been seeing Max's friends invite their whole class to the Gymboree for a party, and you've got a dozen-and-a-half kids hopped up on birthday cake running around and crashing into each other and a few parents crawling into those little colorful snake tubes because somebody got stuck, and every 7.2 seconds somebody is crying, because, let's face it, when you're three years old, there is nothing more natural than to haul off and whack somebody. They're like tiny little Mafiosi: hey, you looking at me? Whap! Hey, isn't that my Kooshball? Smack! Hey, didn't I tell you I get half of all your candy? Whack!

No, we stayed faithful to the very carefully thought-out concept that a kids' party should have as many guests as his age, plus one for good luck. So we invited four kids, who of course came with their four siblings, and of course all the mothers dropped them at our house and took the hell off, so there I was with nine kids of various ages jazzed on birthday cake, bouncing off the walls and smacking each other, and wishing we were someplace with padded walls, like maybe the Gymboree. *"The Longest Day"* is not D-day. It's B-day.

Anyway, along with his third birthday presents came the obsessive behaviors.

Lots of them.

Suddenly, he had to close every open drawer. Every open door. When we got in the car, the sliding console between the seats had to be forward ("Wait! Don't drive! The thingy is back! Move the thingy!") Breakfast was a ritual more complex than opening the Torah: I had to lay everything out in order in the kitchen (pancake, whipped cream, orange juice in an orange sippy cup, milk in a red sippy cup, Batman fork, napkin placed down parallel to the counter's edge), then he had to set the table, during which time I was NOT allowed to set foot in the dining room, or we'd have to start again. And God forbid any of these were even slightly out of order: "No! Daddy! Milk in red sippy cup! Want milk in red sippy cup! No want milk in blue sippy cup!"

"Max, the red sippy cups are dirty. You can drink from a blue cup."

"Noooo! No drink from blue cup! No taste good! Need red cup! Waaaaaahhhhhh!"

And then . . .

. . . there is this moment.

This moment, when your son is collapsed on the floor, his head back, tears streaming down his face, screams and sobs coming in heaves and waves, his inhalations a soggy uh-uh-uh-uh gasp for air, a buildup of incredible tension, released in powerful blasting wails, his very soul writhing in torment, his body twisted and his fists clenched, and you wonder, in your deep-down-dad brain:

Is this worth it?

We are dads. We want order. We want to teach our kids some self-control. We do not want them to be brats who have to get their own way. We know we have to draw the line somewhere.

But is this it? Do we have the great showdown, do we face Armageddon, over a blue sippy cup?

Well, gentlemen, here's what I did.

I caved.

And in caving, I felt like I had achieved what I began thinking of as True Dadditude: the attitude that would let me be the father I really wanted to be.

Let me tell you why.

There is one key difference between dads and moms, other than movie choices on date night.

Moms believe you pick your battles.

Dads don't.

Dads like consistency: If the kid screams, he goes to the time-out chair. If we are consistent about that, he will learn that screaming is wrong.

If the kid fights about bedtime, we sternly tell him that bedtime is bedtime. He will quickly learn that fighting is useless, and will trundle off to bed when told.

If we are not consistent about these things, the kid will learn that if he fights long enough, he will get his way, and chaos will rule, and the house will fall down around us, and we're not insured for that.

Moms are wimps. They think it's OK to cave in, sometimes, just to get through the day.

Now, gentlemen, please do not heave this book out the window when I say this, especially if you live in a building with a doorman, because you might hit him and you're not insured for that either.

But the moms have a point.

See, the problem is, we took just enough psychology in school to learn about B. F. Skinner and his little rats that pushed a lever and got a food pellet, and we learned that behavioral change is a result of stimulus-response reactions.

It's the same principle that's at work with the electric fence that gives dogs a shock every time they get to the end of the yard, so they quickly learn not to leave the yard. My father's joke, which is relevant at this point, went like this:

Guy wags his arm in front of the doctor.

"Doctor, it hurts when I do this."

"So, don't do this."

(Obviously, I know that wasn't really my father's joke. I mean, he told it, but he didn't write it. Obviously, it was written by B. F. Skinner.)

The trouble is, we took just enough psychology to learn about stimulus-response reactions, but when they taught the next part, we were out somewhere getting stoned—or, at least, that's why my generation missed the next part; later generations of dads-to-be were skipping class to sit at their computers day-trading. Either way, generations of future dads must have been out on the day they taught the next part, which was: Intermittent reinforcement is stronger than consistent reinforcement.

I base the theory that all men skipped class that day on the fact that I have never met a dad to whom the theory of intermittent reinforcement makes any sense.

And yet.

There are two reasons for dads to learn the value of intermittent reinforcement. One is, it works. As crazy as it sounds, if the rat only gets the food pellet *sometimes* when he pushes the lever, he becomes obsessed with the lever, and goes after it *all* the time. (Imagine a beautiful woman who sleeps with you every fourth time you ask. You'd hit on her a lot, wouldn't you? Like, probably, four times a day, at least.)

So, as much as we want to trust our Inner Mussolini, there are reasons to learn to go the other way.

I learned this, actually, from watching Jason Giambi hit.

You see, all dads have a great strength, a great power. We can stand steadfast and strong in the face of adversity: We learned this by continuing to go to the same bar, no matter how many times the women there turned us down. Or to the same job, even though our boss was a jerk. It is what we do. We can sternly and resolutely insist that we will not transfer the milk to the red sippy cup, no matter how loudly anyone is screaming, because, how will you ever learn if I give in to your screaming?

And so, we stubbornly parent the way Jason Giambi hits.

Don't get me wrong: Giambi is a powerful hitter. Not as powerful as he was before the steroid scandal, which of course we know and would like to reassure his lawyers that we know he was *not* involved in, but I guess he must have gotten depressed for his friends, because when steroids stopped becoming so available he went into a slump, a sympathy slump, I guess, but still, he's a great hitter.

In his way.

Giambi is such a pure lefty pull hitter that opposing teams put on one of the most dramatic overshifts ever, moving the shortstop over to play short right field, leaving a huge hole between second and third, the poor third baseman having to cover the entire left side of the field. It's all well and good that Giambi can hit the upper deck in right every 18 at bats or so—but when the game's on the line, and all we need is a little bingle to score a man from second, don't you wish he could just poke the ball the other way once in a while? I mean, it's a sure hit. The guy could be batting .400. Don't you wish there were somebody on his team who knew how to hit to the opposite field, and could help him learn?

Oh wait, there is. Derek Jeter. Greatest opposite-field hitter since Rod Carew. Giambi stands in the on-deck circle or on the dugout steps every time Derek bats, and never learns a thing.

So, the point is, you are married to Derek Jeter.

You could learn to go the other way.

Men have power. We have strength. We also have an uncanny ability to sense when a pretty woman has walked out of an office building, but that is less useful at this juncture. No, the great strength we have is our ability to remain consistent and steadfast; it is driven by our need to control. We are driven to control everything. Especially driving. Men like to do the driving, they like the feeling of control. It is why we love stick shifts. The automatic transmission has come a long way since Oldsmobile introduced the Hydra-Matic Drive in 1939, but we disdain it; we will drive it, but we will not feel good about ourselves. No, grabbing that big penis sticking up in the middle of the car and saying, "I and only I will decide when we are ready to enter third gear, and at that time I will do it smoothly and properly"—that is the essence of how we like to drive.

And how we like to parent, too.

Relinquishing control does not come naturally to us. It is a learned behavior. Like hitting to the opposite field.

And so, I hear Max waking up, and I roll over and kiss Derek Jeter, and I go cuddle with Max for a while, and we go downstairs to start our obsessive-compulsive ritual, and in my morning fog I put the milk in the blue sippy cup, and Max wails to the heavens at the wrongness of it all, and I want to use this as a moment to teach him right from wrong and who's the boss and all that. And instead, I cave.

I go wash a red sippy cup. Max stops moaning, intrigued.

I pour the milk into the red cup. He beams. If a three-year-old can gloat, then he is gloating.

I hand it to him. He giggles, and puts the cup to his nose.

"It not full all the way. Fill it all way."

Oy vey.

"No, Max, you never drink that much milk. Drink what's there, and then you can have some more."

"Fill it all way! Fill it all way! Fill it all way! Fill it all way!"

What the hell. I've already shown the wussiness that is my true self, given up the talking stick, relinquished the power gong, purchased an automatic transmission car. I fill the cup. Satisfied, Max places it on the kitchen-counter staging area, lined up in exactly the right position, between the orange juice and the Batman fork, smiles at a universe in which everything now makes sense, and begins setting the table.

I suddenly had a Neil Young song stuck in my head—the one about filling your cup, the one that talks about the promise of a man. And it struck me. Not for a second did I think Neil Young was writing about fatherhood (although he did have a son with Carrie Snodgrass, the actress whom the song is about. Did you know she had a bit part in *Easy Rider*? I think anyone who had a bit part in *Easy Rider* is automatically cool for life. Like having been at Woodstock. Everything about that movie is cool. Except for Peter Fonda. It was his last cool moment. But everything else). The song

"Harvest," inscrutable as most of the lyrics are, is, I think, about the chance of finding true love with crazy women, something many of us spend most of our twenties doing, which is why we liked Neil Young so much when we first heard him. But the line about the promise of a man—that's what I was now stuck on, 30 years later.

Because that's what it's all about, isn't it? Our promise, as a man. Our promise to our daughters, and our sons. How our attitude—our Dadditude—must be a mix of staying true to ourselves, so as to teach our children to be themselves, and of learning to change, to bend, to accept. I was trying to feel right about giving in to Max's tantrum, to believe that this was not just spoiling the child. I was, frankly, torn. And Neil Young wasn't getting me out of this.

But Max interrupted this calm moment of reverie. For one thing, it was time to put whipped cream on his pancakes. For another, he didn't like Neil Young.

"Sing Beatles, Daddy. Sing Beatles. And more whipped cream!"

I did not hesitate to obey.

Soon, this epiphany, this question of whether I could truly find Dadditude—the middle ground between the dad who is firm and teaches discipline and order, and the mom who gives unconditional love and chooses her battles—whether I could win my son's mind and heart at the same time—this question would be put to the test.

Because I was about to fly solo.

Rachel had left us alone for various periods of time before. These usually went fairly well (in the sense that the day Max broke my nose, there wasn't really all that much blood, considering. This is true: he'd decided, in some random quiet moment, that a good way to finish off cuddle time was to launch the back of his head at the bridge of my schnoz. I heard a loud "crack" and the room went purple. In case you are wondering, there are two things you think of in this moment: One, I May Not Pass Out. I Am Alone With The Child. The electricity of this thought zaps you with enough adrenaline to lift a truck. And Two, how am I going to keep it from Rachel that my son can already beat me up?).

Max and I had even made it overnight a few times. But those were sprints; this was long-distance, a real three-day trip, and I would be a real, three-day single dad. She was taking Anna with her; the boys were going to be home alone.

Rachel wrote out instructions for taking care of Max which were just slightly less complex than the rules for that three-dimensional chess game Spock was always staring at (do you notice that we never actually saw him make a move? I think that secretly, Spock didn't know how to play. He just thought the game was a cool way to impress women. He was half-human, after all).

Rachel left instructions on what he should eat, and when; how many bananas to add to his meals if his poops were too loose, and how many raisins if they were too hard (you think I'm making this up. I have saved the envelopes these instructions were written on the back of—people with children are never organized enough to find things like notepads—for when she sues me for libel. Truth, I know from my years as a journalist, is the ultimate defense. That, and really expensive lawyers).

She piled his clothes, outfit-by-outfit, with notes on when he should wear them. She made lists of which ointments work best for which maladies (itchy dry skin, Aquaphor; itchy skin from bug bites, Cortaid; itchy skin from chafing, Balmex—women can parse skin like men can parse Dylan lyrics). I had lists for bath times, bed times, snack times, milk times, orange juice breaks, possible activities—you'd think I had just moved in yesterday. I tossed the lists aside, assuring her that as a fully participatory and committed dad, not to mention one with a new attitude of equanimity, I would discern Max's needs by the same osmosis she did, and respond in kind.

Of course, the moment she left the house, I went Dumpster-diving for the lists, and spent an hour committing them to memory.

Rachel and Anna left early on a Friday morning; as they loaded the car, I reassured my wife that everything would be all right. I was smiling so wide, I looked like the Joker.

And as they pulled away, I walked inside and collapsed on the floor.

I was petrified.

And yet, at the same time, I was elated.

I knew this would mean great bonding time for me and Max, a chance for me to try out my new attitude; I envisioned endless sessions of T-ball, long cuddles in front of the TV, cheerfully peaceful afternoons listening to Bach and making fudge (note to self: how the hell do you make fudge?).

We did not start off on such an idyllic note.

It was time to wake Max up to get him ready for Miss Diane's School. I bravely entered his room, ready to start this adventure.

"Good morning, my darling, darling boy," I cooed.

"I want Mommy," he replied.

I knew better than to get into that trap. I could distract him, I knew, with his favorite treasured clothing. "Mommy is on a trip, remember? Today is a daddy day. We can start by picking your shirt. Do you want to wear your Superman shirt today, or your Yellow Submarine shirt?" This incredible conundrum—the equivalent of, say, asking a Republican senator if he'd rather key Hillary Clinton's car, or give rich people a tax cut—was certain to take his full attention.

"I want Mommy," Max replied.

"Uh, Max, would you like to go down to the Capitol and key Hillary Clinton's car?" It was worth a shot.

"I want Mommy," Max replied.

Strategy one—distraction—mission failure.

Strategy two—direct bribery. "OK, tell you what! Let's go make pancakes, and eat them in front of the TV! And you can put on all the whipped cream! And hey, guess what! I bought some checkerboard ice cream!"

"I want Mommy," Max replied.

Time to go to strategy three: Just haul the kid downstairs and hope for the best.

We made it through our obsessive-compulsive breakfast ritual, the proper liquids in the correctly colored sippy cups. I got Max onto and off of the potty and dressed and out the door, and we had a rollicking good time singing in the car on the way to Miss Diane's. Our family routine was that daddy drops you off and mommy picks you up, but by this time Max appeared to be grokking the fact that mommy was out of the picture and seemed, at least for the moment, to be fine with that. We had somehow turned the corner.

"Give Daddy a hug goodbye," I said. "Remember, Daddy picks you up today. Mommy is in New York City."

"Bye Daddy. Daddy pick me up today. Mommy in New York City. I ride the rocking horse."

I stood, stunned, in the doorway of Miss Diane's, as Max skipped off to ride the 70-year-old rocking horse that served as the Athletics Area, and thought: Hey, I'm good at this!

On the way to the office, I was beaming. Hey, I'm good at this! I am a good father! Very good! I am a single father today and I am doing quite well! My chest puffed up so much it threatened to set off the air bag—hell, it WAS the air bag—and still I crowed: What a good single father am I!

Having given my notice, I was in my final days at *America's Most Wanted*. That morning the newsroom was the usual mix of chaos and coffee and crime, the cable news channels awash with stories of the latest missing child, frantic reporters running into my office to give me updates on whether the cops thought the child was a runaway or a stranger abduction. It was all heavy on my mind as I left at noon to go pick up Max; I thought a lot about that little missing girl as I got my car out of the garage and started driving, the same way I had driven from that garage every single day since we moved our offices into that building two years ago.

I drove home.

I stopped the car, and looked at my empty house, and thought about missing children, and how hard it was to deal with them now that I had Max.

MAX!

I didn't have Max!

Oh my God. I had driven, like a mule on a towpath, the same route I drove every day, all the way home, preoccupied with work, not thinking where I was going—and I forgot to stop and get Max! I spun a tire-screeching U-turn over my neighbor's sidewalk, and floored it in the general direction of Miss Diane's.

I careened around corners with tears in my eyes: I am a bad father! Bad! What a bad single father am I! I have committed the one sin that you are never, never supposed to commit when you are in charge of the child, namely, FORGETTING THE DAMN CHILD ALTOGETHER! All those years of worrying that I would leave him on top of the car and drive away, all those years of having to go check him in his bed at three in the morning, just to make sure that he was still there, all those hundreds of missing kid stories I was faced with—and now *I* was the derelict dad! What if Max was sitting on the sidewalk, crying, holding Miss Diane's hand right at this very moment, as she explained to the policeman about this father who had abandoned his child, and I drove up just as the social worker was taking Max into custody, for his own good, until they could complete their investigation, and I had to tell Rachel that—Oh my God! What would Rachel do when she found out I had FORGOTTEN THE DAMN CHILD ALTOGETHER! This could not be a good thing for our relationship, and would almost certainly undermine my argument that dads are better parents than moms, because I was certain that if I looked it up I would learn that in the history of parenting, no mother had ever FORGOTTEN THE DAMN CHILD ALTOGETHER! Yes, yes there was the Hansel and Gretel incident, but even those parents were actually pro-actively trying to lose the children—until that time, even they had probably never FORGOTTEN THE DAMN CHILD ALTOGETHER!

I was sobbing as I screeched on the brakes in front of Miss Diane's, where I saw, to my utter amazement. . . .

. . . nothing.

I looked at the clock in the car. It was 12:29. Pickup time was 12:30.

I had made it.

I walked down the hill, past the little ceramic hedgehog, as one of the moms walked up, and talked to me through her child, the way parents do: "Look, Caleb, it's Max's daddy! He's coming to pick up Max! Isn't it nice to see Max's daddy! How is Max's daddy doing? He's a single dad today, isn't he?"

"Yes, he is. Max and his daddy are doing just fine," I lied, sweat pouring down my back, my knees shaking, my arms shaking, my underarms working like the sprinkler in Miss Diane's backyard, where I found Max, under a tree, pushing a bulldozer through the sandbox, back and forth, back and forth, over and over.

"Hi Max," I said.

"Hi Daddy. Dis a bulldozer. Massie do a bulldozer. Daddy pick me up today. Mommy in New York City."

"Max, I am an unworthy father, and you are not safe with me, so I am going to ask Miss Diane if you can stay here," I didn't say. I thought it, but I didn't say it. I said this:

"Can Daddy have a hug?"

Max took a moment, torn between the lure of the bulldozer and the request from his daddy, and something in him decided, for once, to break from his obsessive-compulsive behavior, and he put down the bulldozer and came over and put his arms around my neck, and squeezed fresh tears from my eyes.

"I love you, Max," I said.

"Dis a bulldozer, Daddy. Massie do a bulldozer."

I stood him up, and patted him down, and pulled stolen cars from his pockets to his half-hearted protests ("No, I just borrow dem!"), and I put on what I hoped would pass for a nonchalant smile, and waved to Miss Diane, and, hand in hand, Max and I walked up the steep driveway, pausing to pat the little ceramic hedgehog's head. As we drove off, I felt that I had been delivered, saved from a horrible fate, allowed to return to the world of decent people where I really had no business even standing at their shores, let alone walking amongst them, and yet, here I was, stopped at a suburban traffic light, in two lines of perfectly respectable cars with perfectly respectable people in them, and anyone surveying the scene would not suspect that one of them was a very, very bad man, given a second chance for no good reason other than the fact that sometimes, you get lucky.

(If I may take a moment to speak directly to my wife, who has never before heard this story: Rachel, it really wasn't this bad.)

(If I may take a moment to speak directly to the rest of you: Yes, it was.)

"How was the pickup?" the babysitter asked when I finally got home—with Max, this time—to drop him off so I could go back to work.

"Fine! Max understands that Mommy is in New York City, and that Daddy is an idiot who got away with one," I didn't say. I thought it, but I didn't say it.

It was just a few weeks later that I said goodbye to *America's Most Wanted*. I hoped that leaving the world of missing children behind would make me calm down a bit about the little calamities I continued to imagine for Max. As his obsessive-compulsive behavior got worse—and when I say "worse," I don't mean, "As bad as my friend's kid who if you take the wrong shirt out of the dresser, he screams until you take all the rest of the shirts out and put them all back and start again," or, "As bad as my other friend's kid who doesn't go to sleep until midnight because that's how long it takes to get all the cars lined up and then go back down and check to make sure none of them moved when the airplane went over the house"—when I say "worse," I mean quite simply that every behavior anyone exhibited immediately became enshrined in the That's How We Do It Hall of Fame—as his obsessive-compulsive behavior got worse, I struggled to learn the same lesson I kept having to learn, over and over, that you just can't control everything.

More and more, I felt like I was getting the message, from the universe, that no matter how you try to control things, the lesson you have to learn as a father—the Dadditude attitude—was that you can only do what you can, and accept the rest, because you can't control what happens to your child much more than you can control the wind around the sailboat. You can trim the sails and hope for the best (or whatever people with boats do to sails—Jews don't sail, they sink, but I assume the rest of you can fill in this analogy for me)—you can do all that, but the wind is going to do what the wind is going to do.

I finally, finally learned that, the hard way, just a few weeks later.

We were headed off to Atlantic City for a weekend with Max's grandpa and grandma, because, after all, it's never too early for a child to learn you must always, always back up your starting bet at the craps table. My Aunt Dottie and Uncle Artie weren't really Max's grandparents. But since both my parents and Rachel's had long since departed for the great deli in the sky before Max was born, Dottie and Artie were doing an incredible job of filling the grandparent role, which consists mainly of (a) deciding everything the child does is stunningly brilliant and (b) announcing that everything the parent does is basically wrong.

Dottie's main contribution was to get furious anytime I mentioned anything about Max's earlier developmental disabilities, as though by saying Max might be autistic, I was giving God an idea.

What IS it with Jews and their image of God as this lunatic ready to pounce on your every indiscretion? I remember when I was six years old, walking the two miles home from school in the Bronx—actually, that's a lie, I just Googled the directions, and it was less than half a mile, although Google does shorten the trip slightly by telling you to walk on Rochambeau Avenue, which is ridiculous, because that's where that bully Michael lived. And who the hell has bullies named Michael, anyway? Now that really makes you feel like a wimp. At least he could have been named Butch or something. I hate that my bully was named Michael, but that was his name, and if you walked on Rochambeau Avenue, he would most certainly punch you just for the hell of it, face on a bad day, arm on a good one; so the fact that Google directions take you on Rochambeau Avenue instead of the more bully-free DeKalb Avenue route shows that the Internet does have its informational limitations. Anyway, so as I was walking home from school with my mom and Grandma Fagel, I spotted this kid in a wheelchair, and, having trudged what seemed like much more than the half-mile home, I opined out loud that it might be nice to be in a wheelchair, so you didn't have to walk everywhere.

Well, I might just as well have said, "Hey God, I dare you to try and harm me, in fact, why don't you just try right now, let's see what you've got, I bet you can't even hit as hard as that kid Michael on Rochambeau Avenue." Grandma Fagel and my mother started screeching, shouting to the sky in Yiddish, which I understood at the time, and so I know they were saying something along the lines of "Please God, don't listen to him, he's an idiot! We all know you can hit much, much harder than that kid Michael on Rochambeau Avenue! Oy gevalt!"

And so, this fear that God was listening in on your conversations to trap you in some statement you would rue for the rest of your life, like everybody who ever got three wishes in any science fiction story and asked to be the all-powerful ruler of a country and poof they're Hitler in a Berlin bunker in 1945 after the Allied invasion of Germany, or said they wanted to be able to fly and poof, they're a mosquito, screaming "help me help me" in this tiny little voice; this fear is why Dottie freaked out any time I tried to explain why we thought Max wasn't talking—God might hear and get a dumb idea.

Artie's main contribution, on the other hand, was much simpler: teaching Max little Yiddish phrases and demonstrating the fine art of the nap. "I kiss you on the keppie,"

Artie would say, putting his lips to Max's forehead. That, and "Goodnight, Maxelah."

So there we all were in our Atlantic City hotel rooms, getting ready for a night on the town, when I hear a loud thunk from the bathroom. I heard Rachel scream, and I heard Max start wailing, and I ran over to see Max doubled over on the floor. It was clear that he had hit his head on something, and I picked him up and tried to keep everyone calm.

Max's face was buried in my shoulder, and he was screaming to high heaven; I could see white all the way around Rachel's irises as she forced out the words, "I . . . have to . . . see . . . him."

"Rachel, Rachel, calm down," I said, in that great I Am The Calm One voice that dads are such masters of, except when we're not, which is much more often.

"I . . . have . . . to . . . see . . . him," she repeated, and pulled the caterwauling child's face away from my shoulder.

And what we saw was awful.

There was a lump on his forehead about the size of a large Silly Putty egg, blue and white, split down the middle and bleeding profusely. From somewhere far away I heard Rachel's voice explaining that he had been running out of the bathroom, and fell, and cracked his head on the metal door jamb. The giant lump on Max's forehead was the most ghastly and terrifying sight I have ever seen in my life. My knees turned to rubber. I sat down on the bed with Max, and two thoughts erupted from deep within me, filling my consciousness completely, like that moment on acid when the walls start moving.

One was this: So, now I know. Max will grow up to be the man with the big lump on his head. I will love him, my son, my son, my beautiful beautiful son who forever has the giant lump on his forehead, because your father was not careful enough, because I sinned by saying positive things before God without saying kina horah, because I sinned by saying negative things before God and giving him bad ideas, because there is no God and I was not a careful enough father to guide you through a random universe.

The other thought was this: Rachel, call the front desk and tell them we need an ambulance.

The second thought turned out to be the more useful.

There are many advantages to staying in places awash in so much gambling money they don't know what to do with it, so for the hell of it they actually hire enough staff to deal with emergencies. Within seconds, a team of men in black jackets and blue ties and one EMT in an orange jumpsuit were swarming the room, shining flashlights in Max's eyes, giving me ice wrapped in a washcloth, explaining that they had seen this sort of injury often and that it's not as bad as it looks, telling us they had an ambulance waiting downstairs, and that they recommended taking Max to the hospital, but of course that was our decision, right, like we're going to say, "No, thank you, we appreciate the attention, but we think we'll just hang here for awhile and watch TV OnDemand."

It was the second time in our lives—in Max's life—we found ourselves in what seemed a life-threatening situation in a hotel room. You'd think we'd stop traveling by now.

It was also the second time in my life—in Max's life—I saw myself as the father I truly am, and Rachel as the mother she truly is. I don't know where fathers learn to be stoic and calm in a crisis, but somehow, a peace came over me, and I spoke in soft tones to Max, and pressed the ice to his forehead, and kissed him gently, and told him he would be all right. And Rachel sat beside me, one hand pressed on my back, one on Max's, and I knew that the peace that came over me had come from her, and Max stopped screaming, tears just falling silently now, and I knew, whatever might come, that I would indeed always love this boy, that you can control nothing, and that doesn't matter, all that matters is that this boy is here, with me, and I am here, with him: I don't know what it is that makes me love you so, I only know I never want to let you go, 'cause you started something—can't you see? That ever since we met you've had a hold on me? No matter what you do—I only want to be with you.

And when we were all calm and quiet, me Rachel and Max and the men in the black jackets and blue ties, we got up, and our tight, efficient group headed to the locked-and-waiting elevator, through an emergency entrance to a waiting ambulance. We decided Rachel would ride in the back with Max, and as I gently handed him to her, I asked him if he was OK.

His first words, since the accident occurred: he said, with a sob, "My keppie hurts."

This is what it is to be a dad: I helped Rachel down onto the gurney, where she would lie with Max lying on top of her—suddenly, he was smiling: "I ride in ambulance! I ride in ambulance! Put on the siren!"—and then, strong, and stoic, dealing with the situation as efficiently as one can, I walked briskly to the front of the ambulance, and climbed in the passenger seat, and put my hands in my face, and began to cry.

I allowed myself to cry for just 20 seconds. Then, it was time to go back into crisis mode.

Fathers get a bad rap for being able to control our emotions, and maybe we're too good at it for our own good. But this is what fathers do. We go into crisis mode, and turn to the ambulance driver, and say, calmly, let's go.

Atlantic City itself is like the dinner shows in its casinos: They may be all beautiful women and wonderful music and glitter and flash and brilliant magicians, but you wouldn't really want to look backstage. The city's the same: Just a few blocks away from the great façade of the casinos is a depressed, dirty, Jersey shore burg that's already, or still, drunk at four in the afternoon. The incredibly efficient men in the black suits and blue ties left us at the hospital, and now we were not in the protective cocoon of a casino awash in money anymore, we were in the rundown waiting room of a crumbling inner city emergency room on a Saturday night. They had checked Max when he came in, and said he was probably OK—the lump was much smaller, already, and the bleeding had stopped—but they still wanted him to see a doctor, which I knew would mean a wait of several hours, so I held Max in my arms, in a little metal chair, and tried not to make eye contact with the derelicts and drunks around us. I sang his favorite song, "Lucy in the Sky with Diamonds," softly and slowly, and on the third verse, the one about the train station, the drunk next to me, filthy and reeking of gin and cigarettes, leaned toward me and joined in.

Surprisingly, he knew all the words and was perfectly on key. See, you never know.

In the end, it was all fine. The swelling went down, and Max got a Band-Aid and a lollipop (it's nice that, after all these years, some things haven't changed, and the lollipop remains the main currency of survival of all haircuts and doctor visits).

But the odd thing is, everyone—the nurse, the doctor, the guy at the front desk of the restaurant who let us in two hours after our reservation, all my friends after I told them this story—said the same thing.

"Oh, the big egg on the forehead? Yeah, my kid had that. Scary, ain't it?"

Now, I often say to Max, you know Daddy loves you, even when he's angry at you, and I say to all of you now, just because I'm angry at you, doesn't mean I don't love you.

But I am really, really, pissed off.

It turns out, everybody knew about the big-egg-on-the-forehead thing. Well, excuse me, but why didn't somebody say something to me? All those times people came to visit, and cooed at how cute a baby he was, couldn't someone have said, oh, and by the way, sooner or later he will crack his head on something and get a lump the size of a Silly Putty egg; don't worry, it goes away? I mean please, gentlemen, what the hell is the Internet for if not to convey information to each other? Nine times a day someone tells me how to make my penis bigger or refinance my mortgage, I couldn't once get an email saying by the way, don't worry about the egg on the forehead? I will say that I do like the fact that the big penis people and the small mortgage people have now joined forces, and I get those cool emails about how you can get a bigger penis and a bigger house for one incredibly low rate, but only if I click here! I will admit that I once opened one of those how-to-have-a-bigger-penis emails, just out of curiosity, of course. While it was downloading a virus into my computer which would soon turn my C drive into something as useful as a small metal Frisbee, It gave me the following instructions: Rub penis vigorously. Larger penis size guaranteed. Warning: Results may be temporary.

Anyway, I really wish somebody had mentioned something about the differential between gruesomeness and permanence of head injuries. Today, if you look very, very closely, you can see a tiny scar on Max's keppie. It is there as a reminder, to his daddy, that many, many things about being a father are out of your control. You are born with the penis you have, and the luck you have, and you're not going to change either of them for very long.

On the drive back from Atlantic City, we listened to Peter and the Wolf approximately 117 times; the first time Max identified each of the instruments ("That the oboe, Daddy. The oboe is the duck") it was incredible; after a dozen times, mind-numbingly repetitive. But I tried to stay in the moment, the great moment of driving, just over the speed limit, along the Atlantic City expressway, my incredibly calm wife beside me, my son in the backseat with a little Band-Aid on his keppie and no great Silly Putty egg under it; I felt the smooth road under me and reveled in the great feeling you get from holding the steering wheel steady—"Two hands, Daddy," Max would call from the backseat when I would lazily drop an arm to my side—two hands on the wheel, heading for home, the duck is the oboe, grandpa is the bassoon, he gives you a kiss on the keppie and sends you off to sleep, and there's nothing you can change about any of it, whether God is forgiving or spiteful or nonexistent, there is nothing you can do but just keep two hands on the steering wheel, and hope for the best.

8

Autumn, When the Leaves Turn Blue

Earlier on in this book, I made a joke at Oprah Winfrey's expense, which was probably not wise, because now I will never get to go on *Oprah*. I love Oprah; she was great to us at *America's Most Wanted*, and she was actually responsible for one of our biggest captures. We'd been chasing a good-looking, well-to-do international playboy named John Hawkins, a bisexual former model who would have actually been a very cool guy except for the fact that he and his lover concocted an insurance fraud scheme that, unfortunately, required an actual dead body, which appears to have been obtained from a doctor, who appears to have produced the dead body by killing its owner. We were never able to catch the guy, even though our reenactment had actual sex scenes in it. But when John Walsh went on Oprah to complain about not being able to catch the guy, somebody in Italy was watching her show, and called in a tip which we knew was a good one, because she knew a certain anomaly about Mr. Hawkins' penis that one of his gay lovers had already told us about, although we had left it out of our reenactment, even in the sex scenes, because we knew it would be a good tip to watch out for, and we didn't want to give it away. Penis anomalies are always good tips: this is one of the details of forensic science you don't hear about on *CSI: Miami* as often as you'd think. I probably shouldn't reveal the nature of the penis anomaly, because even people convicted of conspiracy to commit murder have a right to some modicum of privacy, and revealing that someone has a penis anomaly without revealing what it is constitutes, I believe, the dictionary definition of "modicum."

So, the tip from Oprah's viewer caught John Hawkins, and after that we had a great relationship with Oprah's show, and she had John Walsh on many times to help search for missing children, and that's why I'm sorry I blew the relationship by passing a remark about Oprah earlier, about her being responsible for all the bad press that dads get, which I guess I could have gone back and deleted, or changed, but you wanted the truth, so there it is.

I would have liked to go on *Oprah*, because I think I have good advice to pass along to other dads, although those of you who have read this far will probably dispute that, and I'd be hard pressed to argue. Nevertheless, since I will never get to go on *Oprah*, I thought I would share an excerpt of the interview that would have happened, had I not blown the opportunity. Here, then, is what Oprah and I never got to say to each other:

Oprah: Welcome to the show!

Me: Thanks, and may I say, you look marvelous. Have you lost some weight?

Oprah: Thanks for noticing! Yes, (*turning to the audience*) in the last six months I have lost FORTY-SEVEN POUNDS! (*Great applause.*) AGAIN! (*Greater applause.*)

Me: That's wonderful.

Oprah: You could lose a little weight yourself, you know. Bread is the enemy.

Me: I'll try to remember that.

Oprah: Now tell us, your book makes the startling allegation that fathers are, in some ways, more caring than mothers are.

Audience: Booo! Hisss! Other negative sounds!

Me: Well, it's like this, Oprah. May I call you Oprah?

Oprah: We'll see. Depends on your answer. Please continue.

Me: It's just that I think fathers have an immense need to bond with their children, especially in the first year. We don't have the natural bond that moms have just by the nature of nature, so we work harder at trying to bond. By virtue of our hard work, we establish our own special relationship with the baby. It's something to conquer. Men like conquering things. Just look at the invasion of Normandy, or understanding the rules for icing the puck.

But women don't get what we're doing. They think we're lousy at bonding with babies, and we tend to believe the hype, so it becomes a self-fulfilling prophecy, and we stay in the background until the kid is old enough to understand fart jokes, at which time we have a distinct advantage over mothers, who don't know nearly as many fart jokes as we do.

Oprah: Can you tell us one?

Me: Well, there you go, see, only a woman would ask that. Men know that when you tell a fart joke, it's not funny. It's only funny when you actually perform one at an inappropriate moment, like in the bathtub, or during parent-teacher conferences. That's comedy.

Oprah: Is there any other advice you can share?

Me: Just this: Fathers do tend to be control freaks, and they measure their success as parents with how well their kids behave. But I've been trying to learn the lesson my son has been teaching me: that you really can't control everything, and that's OK. You can try to set some standards for behavior, which of course will not work, and if you can just learn to laugh at your failure rather than get pissed off about it, you'll have a much happier time of it.

Oprah: So, you need to learn to laugh at things that would normally upset a person.

Me: Exactly.

Oprah: Like farts.

Me: Precisely!

Oprah: And your son is teaching you this lesson.

Me: He's trying.

Oprah: He teaches you by example, or he actually tells you this?

Me: He tells me this.

Oprah: Excuse me, but is this just a way to segue into your next chapter?

Me: Yes, Oprah, I'm afraid it is.

Oprah: You may call me "Miss Winfrey."

✁

Max was three years and a few months old when it came time to leave the friendly confines of Miss Diane's basement and enroll in school.

School!

All right, it was preschool, and it was only three hours a day—but it was every day, and it had the word "school" written right on the front of the building, so there was no mistaking it. We had enrolled Max in a nice little private school a few minutes from our home (its motto: "Way more expensive than Miss Diane's!"); I only wanted him to go to a three-day school, but Rachel did one of those things women can do to men—"They like the routine," she said, as though women have been doing this for years and know everything, and men have just decided to get involved recently and have so much to learn, and . . . Well, OK, that may be true, but they don't have to be so smug about it.

The night before school started, I had that sick feeling in my stomach, which I recognized immediately, not just from the year before, when Max started Miss Diane's School, but something much deeper, something I knew as the Ed Sullivan Blues. This was the feeling you had as a kid on Sunday nights at 8:30 when *The Ed Sullivan Show* would reach the long commercial break that told you the show was half-over, and you knew that bedtime was rushing at you like a tumbling Italian gymnast or one of the other ridiculous acts that would appear between Rosemary Clooney singing "Come On A My House" and the comedy stylings of Marty Allen and Steve Rossi (and how the hell did it come to happen that "Come On A My House" was written by, of all people, William Saroyan, the great American poet, author, and playwright, and Ross Bagdasarian, the great American creator of

Simon, Theodore, and Alvin, the singing chipmunks? Turns out Saroyan and Bagdasarian were cousins. Who knew? I can just imagine their mothers getting together. "My son just won the Pulitzer Prize and the New York Drama Critics Award for 'The Time of Your Life.'" "Well, MY son can speed up his voice so he sounds like a chipmunk." "MY son wrote the immortal line, 'Try to learn to breathe deeply, really to taste food when you eat, and when you laugh, laugh like hell; try to be alive, you will be dead soon enough.'" "Well, MY son wrote the immortal line, 'And then the Witch Doctor, he told me what to do, he said now, ooh, eee, ooh-aah-aah, ting-tang, walla-balla-bing-bang.'" Those must have been some fun Christmas dinners). But as *The Ed Sullivan Show* wore on, you would pray for one more act, anything, a dancing bear, or Ezio Pinza singing "Some Enchanted Evening," or even the June Taylor Dancers, anything to stave off bedtime, because when Ed would come on and list who was going to be on next week's show, you knew you'd hear, "Fivelah, it's time for bed"—that was my Yiddish name, Fivel—and there was no denying the inevitable, there was no more joy to be had, the endless joy of the weekend, there was only the sad march to bed, and sleep, and school the next day, and homework you hadn't done, and hoping that that bully Michael wouldn't find you at recess.

And now, this Sunday night 40 years later, I had that same sour fluttering feeling in my stomach, for Max, because the endless weekend that had lasted for three-and-a-half years was over, and tomorrow was school. It was the biggest case of Ed Sullivan Blues I'd ever had.

Max, for his part, was excited about the start of school. Before bed, I explained to him what the ritual for the next day would be, how he would meet his class in the hall ("OK. Daddy, what's a hall?"), how Daddy would drop you off and Mommy would pick you up. The next morning, he popped out of bed, and we completed the pancake ritual and potty break, and Max put on his giant fire engine back-pack, and walked down the front stairs and turned and said, "Come on, Daddy," and he seemed so much older than he had the day before, and I felt so much older, too.

School is a funny place for a dad to show up. Mostly, it was moms taking the kids into school, and a few dads in shirts and ties quickly dropping their kids off in the car pool line, but hell, I didn't have anywhere else to go, so I walked Max into school. The place was teeming with chil-dren, which is not surprising, it being a school and all, but it freaked me out. First, it bothered me that there was no giant fence around the place—what if Max decides to wan-der off? They have so many kids to tend to. How could they possibly notice if one was missing? And then there was the realization that, even in this hoity-toity private school, there are still ten times as many kids as adults, meaning at any given moment nine children do not have the undivided attention of a grownup. What could happen? I looked around. There was danger everywhere.

Stairs—they have stairs here? Why don't they make schools ranch-style? I've never let Max walk down the stairs without holding his hand, warning him of the dangers of staircases, and tying a restraining rope to him just in case. But here—kids were walking down stairs all by themselves! Running, even! And what's this—paint? They let the chil-dren use paint! Paint looks just like juice! How could Max possibly tell the difference? Do they have a special phone number to call for cases of paint poisoning? Why isn't that number painted directly on the paint cans? It's not like they couldn't find any paint! And everywhere I looked, older children were wielding . . . weapons! Look, there, that kid has a block! He could throw it and take somebody's eye out! And crayons! You could stuff one in somebody's nose and rupture a blood vessel! And, my God, out there on the playground—climbing equipment! Children were perched dangerously high—six, seven feet off the ground! They could fall, and land on one of the kids holding a block and a crayon! And the doors—they all have latches! I've already seen what can happen with latches—why do you need to latch these doors anyway? Kids are running in and out, so you clearly don't lock them while school is open, and what's the point of locking them when school is closed, it's not like some crackhead is going to come in here looking for Tonka trucks he can hock to get a fix. Lose a latch, save a keppie, I thought.

But I was finally distracted from these morbid thoughts by a much more obvious aspect of school: now that all the dads had dropped off their kids, I was surrounded by women.

Women, everywhere. The teachers were women, the lady at the desk was a woman, the moms were most definitely women. This was like your dream bar, only it was daytime and they weren't serving drinks yet, but still, you couldn't help but notice, all those women in those cute morning-mommy outfits: no one shows up for carpool in schleppy bathrobes and curlers. It's all Spandex and leggings, like the June Taylor dancers had made it off *The Ed Sullivan Show* and were hanging around the school yard.

This, I thought, was not all bad.

The kids started the day outside, so we gathered at the edge of the playground for a while to watch, me and the June Taylor dancers, and I began realizing that one of the other great perks of being an involved dad is, women find it endearing that you are taking responsibility for your child. As a result, they don't find you threatening. The playground is the only place you can walk up to a woman tending to her children and say, "excuse me, but they are just adorable," and she does not assume you are talking about her breasts. Even though, of course, you are.

I was worried, after a while, that if I stayed too long I would be perceived as one of those "helicopter parents"— that's what the parenting magazines call moms and dads who hover at school—so after floating a respectable three feet over Max's head for just twenty minutes or so, I alit next to him and told him to give me a hug goodbye.

"Daddy drop me off. Mommy pick me up," Max said, and with that, he was off to class, off to school, off to a world without me.

Bye, Maxie.

The world changes enormously once your kids are in school and you do not have a real job. For one, you find yourself alone with your wife at home at 9:30 in the morning, and you pour a cup of coffee, and languorously read *The New York Times* together, offering each other wonderful bon mots from Frank Rich and R. W. Apple Jr., my my my, they do go on, don't they though, and as your wife reaches over to playfully feed you the last bite of a cinnamon croissant with apricot glaze, you notice how lovely she looks wearing only your lightly starched white button-down shirt, and as it falls open at the collar you flirtatiously utter the single phrase, "Again, mon amour?" And she smiles as her hand lightly caresses your. . . .

Oh, sorry. That wasn't me, that was an ad for Folgers on The Oxygen Channel. My house was a little different.

The chaos level, for some reason, diminished just slightly in the hours the kids were at school; Rachel and I would see each other in passing, frenzied and distracted by our respective searches for freelance gigs and Anna's history paper, which Anna has called on her cell phone from school to announce that she forgot to print out, so could one of us go e-mail it to her RIGHT NOW, and the cleaning lady's cell phone, which is ringing somewhere but none of us can find it (and you're wondering, why would a woman from El Salvador have "Hava Nagilah" as a ringtone, anyway?), which is all the more difficult because of the roof repair guy's hammering away (Rachel, is he supposed to be smashing the tiles like that?), and the dog barking at the ghost of a cat that has apparently taken up residence under the couch, which you can't really deal with right now because Anna is on the phone yelling "No, the OTHER history paper," so we barely have time for the coin flip to see who does the breakfast dishes.

And before you know it Rachel has brought Max home from school, and you have the following fascinating conversation:

ME: Max! How was your first day of school!
MAX: Good.
ME: What did you do?

MAX: I don't know.
ME: Did you make any friends?
MAX: I don't know. Daddy, why don't you have any hair?

In the weeks that followed, the information Max brought home from school would increase a bit. Max was coming home with words and phrases and ideas not actually taught to him by us: Sometimes endearing ("I love my friend Jonathan. Jonathan is cool. He has cool light-up shoes"), sometimes confusing ("The planets live on earth are running no running they eat light"—who the hell is teaching this class, e.e. cummings?), but, mostly, scatological.

It turns out, Max has learned, that his father is, in fact, a poopyhead. With a poopyface. We are not eating breakfast, we are eating poopy. This rocket ship? That's a poopy rocket ship. Hello, Max; hello, poop. Let's sing "Itsy Bitsy Spider": The poopy poopy poopy climbed up the poopy poopy. Max started using "poop" the way my old boss used another four-letter word: Noun, verb, adjective, adverb, preposition, conjunction.

I hired a sherpa guide to get me to the top of the pile of parenting books in the living room, and got caught in the deep crevasse between the two schools of thought on this matter: Ignore it, and don't.

Apparently, your choices on the poopy issue seem to range between don't-react-because-that's-what-they-want-and-it-will-only-result-in-more, and the contrary point of view, which is, stop this immediately, because who the hell wants to hear a kid running around yelling "Poop-man to the rescue!" (Actually, I did kind of like that one.)

We came up, I think, with an ingenious compromise.

I told Max that he was allowed to use the word "poop" all he wanted—but only in the bathroom. This, for some reason, seemed like a grand idea to Max. We immediately went into the potty, and had a long discussion on why poopies poop, you poopyhead, no, you are a poopyhead, no, you are—

—and that was it. This went on for a few days; whenever Max felt the urge to discuss the matter, we headed for the potty, and laughed, and said "poop" a lot, and took care of some business as long as we were in the neighborhood, and Max seemed satisfied.

And I felt like, hey, this parenting stuff is getting easier.

You get to tell yourself that once in a while. It's the illusion that keeps you going.

In fact, the exact opposite is true, because when you have a child, you have to face the realization that Everything Is Much Harder Than You Used To Think. For example, notice this: Dads walk around with their shoes untied a lot. You look at them and think, doesn't that guy know how to tie his own damned shoes? How good a father can he be?

But this is how it goes. One day, after winning the war on "poop," I bend down to tie my shoes (which are a lot farther away than when I was younger, anyway). Max is reaching for a knife. "No! Knives are bad!" I find myself saying, as I leap across the kitchen, protecting the child from the knife with the approved parental method of impaling my palm on it. I remove it and try tying my shoe again. "Dis not a knife!" Max says gleefully, grabbing, of course, another knife. Where did all these knives come from all of a sudden? Who did my wife hire as a housecleaner, Norman Bates?

So there's Max, doing his best Crocodile Dundee imitation ("Dat not a knife, Daddy! Dis a knife!")—and there's me, stumbling after him with my shoes untied, and now he's on a ladder trying to change a lightbulb—where did the LAD-DER come from, for Chrissakes?—and suddenly I'm in some strange French surrealist film with random images popping up at will (why is there a chaise longue in the foyer?), chasing Max around the house, trying to avert disaster, trying to wrest some measure of control out of this moment, and I re-member the shoelaces, having just stepped on my left one with my right foot, which sends me sprawling onto the chaise longue, from which vantage point I can hear Max calling from the playroom, "Look, Daddy, a chain saw!"

—or at least, that's how it feels, when you're trying to do something simple, like tie your shoes, cook a hamburger, or change a lightbulb, around a three year old. You circle the kitchen, opening the coffee on the first pass, measuring it out on the second, turning on the coffeemaker on the next pass, spilling the water on the next—so that the break to go to the potty and tell poopy jokes comes as an enormously welcome relief.

But soon, poopy jokes gave way to more sophisticated humor, as Max started working on the most important thing little boys want to know—besides, of course, how to turn every object in the world into a gun, which seems to come naturally—which is what, exactly, constitutes "funny."

Girls try to figure this out as well, but you can see that they understand, innately, that this is a sidelight for them. Boys understand, innately, that this will become a full-time job. If you doubt me, go ask a few friends to tell you a joke.

Some of them will say, "Oh, gracious, I can't tell jokes." These, of course, will most likely be women. Others will say, "A rabbi, a priest, and the Dalai Lama are in a space-ship, when somebody farts. The Dalai Lama says . . ." These, of course, will most likely be men, because women, bless their hearts, could never get past the question of what the rabbi, the priest, and the Dalai Lama are doing in a space-ship, while men understand that this premise is already fun-nier than most of the jokes they have been sent over the Internet.

My Aunt Dottie doesn't tell jokes, but she e-mails me every joke she finds on the Internet. My favorite one she sent me was stolen from Stephen Wright: "I went to a restau-rant with a sign that said they served breakfast at any time. So I ordered French toast during the Renaissance."

Max did not get this joke, but he did start telling a joke of his own, which, for his age, was not terrible:

"What is a cow's favorite place to go?"

"I don't know, Max, what is a cow's favorite place to go?"

"To the mooooooo-vies!"

Now, here's the thing with kid jokes. You have to laugh, because you want them to have positive reinforcement for trying, but if you laugh, it tells them the joke is funny, which means they want to tell it again. And again. And again. Then they want you to tell it to them, only they guess the punch line (surprise!), which they find hysterical, so funny in fact that their only possible response is to tell the joke a few more times. Max and I have spent entire car rides doing nothing but telling this joke, over and over until my ears bleed.

If that's not unconditional love, I don't know what is.

On this particular morning, I have cut Max's pancake in the acceptable pattern (six cuts vertically, five horizontally, using my own knife and fork, which may not be placed on the table until Max is seated and his chair is pushed in just far enough but NOT TOO FAR!). We have started the pattern of whipped cream placement, which of course is Max-Daddy-Max-Daddy-Max, and the pattern of eating, which, as he has for the previous hundred mornings, since the teachers taught the concept of patterns, Max announces in a loud, clear voice.

"Cream number one, pancakes number two," he intones, solemnly. Meaning the first thing we do is eat the whipped cream, and the second is to eat the pancakes. This is, apparently, the natural order of things.

"Hey Max," I venture, just to shake things up, "today, let's do cream number four, pancakes number five."

Well, you'd think Henny Youngman had come back from the dead and told the joke about the guy who comes home to find the car in the living room ("Guy asks his wife, how did you get the car in the living room?" "Easy, I took a left at the kitchen." But of course you knew that).

Max was hysterical. "Cream number four pancake number five!" he cackled. "That's funny!" He took a bite of cream, but was laughing so hard, it dribbled down his chin.

"Then tomorrow," I said, "We'll do cream number six, pancakes number seven!"

Max stopped laughing. His face became dead serious. "That's not funny, Daddy."

I was insulted. Who was Max to tell me what was funny and what was not? Was I not the man who *wrote* "Cream number four pancakes number five"?

Still, as I tried to tell Oprah in the interview we never had, you can't argue about what's funny. Either something's funny or it isn't, and I was glad Max was learning that lesson, in his own way, at such a young age. He's actually a pretty good-looking kid, so he may become one of those boys who can get girls without being funny, but you can't count on that. Better to give them all the tools they might need in life, and figure out later which ones are most necessary.

At about this time, Max developed three distinct personalities that we began calling the Three Phases of Eve. These phases are known in psychology circles as No, Why, and Bloogle.

The "No" phase was his favorite. Sometimes he'd get stuck in this one for days. It was like getting stuck inside Monty Python's Argument Clinic Sketch. ("This isn't an argument, this is just contradiction." "No it isn't." "Yes it is!" "It is not." "Look, you just contradicted me!" "No I didn't.") I didn't even know Max knew John Cleese, but there you go, and we were in the middle of it.

Max, here are your pancakes ("No no no! I want popcorn for breakfast!"). Sorry, you've got pancakes. Try to use your fork to eat that—"No no no, no want fork." OK, you can use your hands. "No no no, no want hands." Fine. Eat it any way you want. "No no no, I don't want to do whatever I want." Do you need to go to the potty? "No no no." Read a book? "No books." Nap? "Fuggedaboudit." "Max, if you don't stop arguing, you're going to have a time out."

"No want time out! No no no!" "Max, look, here's ten dollars, an ice cream cone, a new car, and a baseball bat you can smash in the television set with. Anything you want. Will you just stop saying no no no?" "No, no no."

This was a tough phase (no it wasn't!), a really tough one (no no no, it was an easy one!), and we tried to weather it as best we could (no you didn't! You tried to weather it very badly!), with a combination of firmness and understanding (no! you can't combine firmness and understanding!). But mostly we had no choice but to wait it out (no! You wait it in!).

More frustrating, if you can imagine it, was the Why phase, because this one was so insidious. It would creep up on you, engulfing you before you knew it. You'd be having a pleasant daddy-time one minute, and the next, you're trapped in the endless loop of logic. At least once an evening, I'd find myself stuck in *My Dinner With Socrates*:

MAX: Daddy, why is your shirt red?
ME: This shirt is red because I bought a red shirt.
MAX: Why did you buy a red shirt?
ME: Because I like red shirts.
MAX: Why do you like red shirts?
ME: Um, I don't know, I just do.
MAX: Why do you just do?
ME: I don't know, Max.
MAX: Why do you not know?
ME: I don't know why I don't know.
MAX: Why do you don't know why you don't know?

It was an inescapable form of torture.

ME: Max, I don't want to talk about my shirt anymore.

MAX: Why do you not want to talk about your shirt anymore?

ME: Because I want to talk about race cars.

MAX: Why do you want to talk about race cars?

ME: Because they're cool.

MAX: Why are they cool?

There was no exit from this conversation. I decided to lay down the law.

ME: Max, you must stop asking why.

MAX: Why do I have to stop asking why?

ME: Because Daddy wants to give you a hug.

MAX: Why does Daddy want to give me a hug?

ME: So you'll stop talking.

MAX: Why do you want me to stop talking?

ME: Because you are making Daddy doubt his very sanity.

MAX: Why does Daddy doubt his very sanity?

ME: Because I thought you were my little Maxie, but it turns out that you are actually René Descartes in a Beatles haircut.

MAX: Daddy, Descartes tell us that if you would be a real seeker after truth, it is necessary that at least once in your life you doubt, as far as possible, all things.

ME: Max, is that really true?

MAX: I doubt it.

And the Why Phase, of course, was a walk in the park, compared to the onset of Bloogle. Bloogle is the most severe form of torture a child can inflict on a parent, and the only cure for it is puberty, so you're in this for the long haul: Max, at random moments, would become a stark-raving idiot.

He would be performing a simple human-child task, such as setting the table in the correct order, when suddenly, he would start jumping up and down on the couch, from which perch he would announce: "Bloogle! Blaaah! Waga-waga-waga!"

"Max, calm down, we're setting the table now."

"Bloogle! Blaaaah! Waga-waga-waga!" he would shout, louder, in case you didn't hear him the first time, and, to emphasize the point, throw his pancake plate toward the ceiling.

"Max! There is no throwing! This is a bad thing! Do you hear that I am using my Voice of Control, to let you know I am serious? Stop this now!"

"Raaaaaaaaaaaaaaga!" Max is now shouting, running toward me, and, just for good measure, giving me a head-butt in the stomach, which, at this age, he can do with enough force to make my eyes bulge out.

Now, please understand that I was not without my weapons. At this point, I knew it was time to pull out the big guns.

"Max, you have two choices," I said calmly. "You can pick up your pancake, or you can have a time-out. Which do you choose?"

According to my mountain of parenting books (which had by now been given its own zip code), giving him a choice allowed him some measure of control and independence. This, they said, is an essential part of forging his personality.

This, however, didn't always work.

"I choose bloogle!" he said, kicking me hard in the shin.

Too much independence and control, apparently.

"Max!" I said, more sternly. "You may not kick Daddy. Now you have a time-out."

This, apparently, is the funniest thing I have ever uttered. He is now laughing so hard that tears are streaming down his face. I repeat my threat; the second time, my timing must have been better, because now he is laughing so hard he can barely speak. He's speed-dialing his friends: "Natalie, you MUST come over here right now. My dad is doing the FUNNIEST bit EVER. No, I'm serious, it's Lenny Bruce meets Robin Williams, truly inspired, I can't describe it, it must be experienced first-hand. Jump on the Big Wheel this instant and get your silly butt over here, girlfriend."

I am astounded by this, because how could he possibly be having this conversation? It's only a toy cell phone. But undaunted, I decide that it's time to draw that line in the sand. It is time to go nuclear.

"Max, you have two choices. You may go to your time-out chair, or I will take away Lightning McQueen. Which do you choose?"

Suddenly, silence.

Lightning McQueen, for the uninitiated, is the star of Pixar's animated *Cars*, a movie populated by talking automobiles, which for Max would be the equivalent of, oh, I can't even imagine what I would like as much anymore— Bob Dylan singing the National Anthem at the Women's Topless Baseball Championship, say. *Cars* was my first experience of the effectiveness of marketing to children— months before the movie came out, we had seen the trailer, listened to the soundtrack, and gone to the Web site where we could hear each of the cars speak; we had purchased the *Cars* place mat and pajamas and toothbrush; we had read the picture book and the chapter book and the coloring book and the *Flo's Drive-In Diner Cookbook*.

We now owned every car in the collection—but of course, Lightning McQueen was the crown jewel, the Rosetta stone, the ounce of pure.

"Max, I said you have two choices," I repeated, softly. "You may go to your time-out chair, or I will take away Lightning McQueen. This is your last chance, or I will choose for you. Which do you choose?"

His shoulders slumped, his face fell. "I choose time-out," he said, sadly, and walked off to the brown chair in the corner of the dining room, to sit, all alone.

"When you are ready to say you are sorry for throwing your pancake and kicking Daddy, you may come out," I said, in an even tone.

I busied myself with cleaning up the mess in the kitchen, feeling smart and competent. This is how a parent handles things, I thought. Calmly but forcefully. Now Max understands that he must listen.

I felt, once again, in control.

And it felt absolutely lousy.

I realized that a moment ago, this kitchen was filled with shrieks of laughter and joy; granted, it was also filled with flying pancakes and body blows, but you have to admit—it *was* funny. Now, the house is silent, and a boy is stifling a sob.

I went over to Max's time-out chair, and knelt down, and gave him a hug.

"I sorry, Daddy," he said.

"That's OK, Max. You just were having fun. Let's go have breakfast."

"I set the table! I set the table! You no set!" Max had rebounded instantly, and was running off to his favorite task.

As he went through his table-setting ritual, I wondered about the events that had transpired that morning. Was it all really worth it? Was the lesson he learned worth the sadness it engendered?

It was a question that was going to come back to haunt me, very soon, big-time.

A few days later, when I went to pick Max up from school, one of the teachers took me aside. They told me that the children had been drawing, but Max wouldn't draw, because he decided his crayons were rocket ships. When they told him he had to do what he was told, he started to cry, and they thought we should know.

The next day—in fact, every day after that—when I picked Max up from school and asked him how his day was, he said the same thing: "I did every thing the teacher said, and I didn't cry."

Oy vey.

This, I knew, was my fault.

Our desire to control our children's behavior, for their own good, too easily slips over the line to controlling their behavior for *our* own good. It's just easier to get through the day—in the car, out of the car, through the checkout line—if you are not in the company of the Tasmanian Devil. But this ease of motion that is borne of a child's compliance comes at a great, great cost.

The price is the feeling of freedom and creativity and joy that, if you are very lucky, your child is born with, and if you are very, very lucky, you will not squeeze all the life out of too soon.

We had a sit-down with the teachers, to talk about how maybe we were all putting too much pressure on this imp, and we all eased off a bit. I thought we were striking a good balance.

But then came the blue leaves.

Max and I got home from school one day, and we were sitting on the floor, having our cookie. I asked him what happened at school that day. To my surprise, I got this:

"I got in trouble."

"Why did you get in trouble, Max?"

"We paint leaves. I want to paint blue leaves. The teacher said dere are no blue leaves."

Oy vey, again.

I hoped this was going to pass, but on the way to school the next morning, Max called to me from the backseat: "Daddy, I just saw two blue leaves."

And the next day: "Daddy, I just saw two more blue leaves."

And the next. And finally, through my thick daddy skull, I understood.

It is not about control. It is not about teaching. It is not about setting boundaries. It is not about limits. It is not about the time-out chair, or offering choices. It's not about any of those things.

Dadditude is just about learning to Be. Here. Now.

"Yes, Max," I said, tilting the rearview mirror down, so I could see his face. "I saw them too. I saw two blue leaves. They are beautiful. They are my favorite."

"They are my favorite too!" he said, with a smile as big as the sun. "I love the blue leaves!"

The school year passed, more meetings with the teachers—who, I must say, knew a lot more about this than anyone I ever knew, and led me through the paces of how to give up some control without the house falling down around you. The same day we told them about the blue leaves, in fact, Max decided he was going to wear his backpack in the front, just for the hell of it.

"Max," the teacher told him, "I like that you do things your own way."

Max glowed, and strode toward the door, bursting with pride. Of course, with his backpack in front of him, it wasn't easy going. But he'll figure that out in his own time.

It was toward the end of the school year that Max came home, and I sat down on the kitchen floor with him for our usual moment of cookie-and-no-information.

"How was school today, Max?"

"Well, we planted seeds," Max told me. "But we didn't put them anywhere. Tomorrow, we put them somewhere. Some of the seeds go in the dark, where they won't grow. Some seeds go in the light, where they will grow. I hope I get to put mine in the light. I want it to grow. Of course, you have to water it. I want to go in the playroom now and play with my cars. Is that OK, Dad?"

And I said, "Excuse me, when did you learn English?"

And that was it. It happened, just like that.

One day, we are amazed that he can distinguish da-da from dog poop; the next, that he can name the planets, sing "Eensy Weensy Spider," form as complex a thought as "I saw two blue leaves."

And one afternoon, they learn to speak, and to think, and to converse.

The very next morning, after the elaborate table-setting ritual, we were about to start our preordained, never-stray-from-it pattern of taking turns putting whipped cream on the pancakes.

Max became unusually pensive.

"Today," he announced, "I want the pattern to be Max-Max-Max-Max-Max."

"Max," I answered, a bit astonished, "the pattern is always 'Max-Daddy-Max-Daddy-Max-Daddy'!" Even I, to my surprise, had become fixated on this ritual.

Max looked me right in the eye, and said, in a measured, even tone: "Daddy, you have to learn to try new things."

What a breakthrough! Perhaps, just like that, it was all over, I thought. The rituals, the obsessive-compulsive door slamming, the refusal to eat anything outside the Seven Approved foods (pancakes, whipped cream, hot dogs, macaroni-and-cheese, ice cream, orange juice, Go-GURT), all of that was about to change. You have to learn to try new things, Max had said, all on his own. My my my. They grow up so fast, and they grow up in their own time, don't they.

"Yes Max," I said, in my most fatherly tone, tousling his hair—I was never much of a hair-tousler, but this seemed like a particularly tousle-appropriate moment. "Yes, my son, you have to learn to try new things."

"No!" he said angrily. "*You* have to learn to try new things. Not me. *You.*"

Well, so maybe they don't grow up as fast as all that.

Still, I had to admit, this was not the same child. Something fundamental had shifted in the universe. You wake up one morning, and the lunacy of the three-year-old is gone, and in its place you have an actual kid, a kid you can teach the rules of baseball to, a kid who can help you clear the table, follow the plot of *The Wizard of Oz*. The kid every father waits for, the child companion on all your adventures.

It is very, very exciting.

And very, very sad.

Goodbye, Maxie.

Hello, Max.

I can't believe you are four years old. It all went by so fast. That little monkey that hung on me, that communicated only with his eyes and his smiles and his frowns and his tears, by pointing and grunting and jumping and lying down—he is gone. And that crazy lunatic who drove me bananas—he's gone too. I love you more than words can tell, my big man, and I think that's why I'm a little sad, because I will never have words that work as well as when we had no words.

But there is great consolation, now, in the great relief of having you to talk to. I've tried to sing you that John Sebastian song, although, much to my surprise, you seem to have fallen in love with rap music. Whenever we flip past it on the radio you say, "I like that one!" and we have to stop. I've been trying to share my music with you, all of your little life—but I guess it's your turn to share yours with me. I hope someday you'll forgive me that when we heard that rap song about all the places the singer wanted to "do it" with his girlfriend, and you asked me what they were going to go do, I said "eat their vegetables." Parents lie sometimes, but we do it out of love.

We make up such complicated stories together, now, and such fun games. You like us to be superheroes, and root out the bad guys. Today you drew me a picture: "This is our home," you said, "but it's really our castle. I drew the door the same color so the bad guys can't find it. I made the road with lots of loops so the bad guys will get lost."

This is what God has given me, for taking away my little monkey. He has given me this friend, who will help me be a superhero, and, of course, avoid the bad guys. So go get dressed, my big man. I have tickets to the ball game today. I have always dreamed of taking you out to the ball game.

And you know what?

I don't care if we ever get back.

So let's go out to the ball game. I think you're ready.

I think I am, too.

9

Nothing But the FAQs

So, that about brings you up to present day, and it occurs to me that I could have been more helpful. I actually have learned a few useful things about surviving daddyhood, which I should have passed along, but I was distracted by the noise coming from the next room, where Max is experimenting with how hard you can throw a toy truck at the wall before either the truck or the wall is destroyed (at which point, he will skulk into my office, head down, and he will ask, "Daddy, my truck broke. Can you fix it?" and I will fix it, because that is what dads do, after which he will gleefully start tossing it against the wall again).

I should go stop him from this activity, but before I do, I would like to pass along some helpful hints about dealing with a four-year-old, because I think I owe you that much. I will present them in handy Q-and-A form, which I learned during my stint at *USA Today*, where we liked creating Q-and-A's for everything, since we got to write the Q's as well as the A's, so as to ensure nobody asked us anything we couldn't answer.

Q: My child is given to terrible tantrums in public. It's very embarrassing. What can I do?

Going deaf is the preferred option for most fathers. Looking at any nearby adult and saying, loudly, "Having a little trouble controlling your child, eh?" is also useful, and even better if you can do this in a plausible foreign accent.

However, it's a lot like your automobile. The question is not really what to do in case of a breakdown—it's more important to know how to prevent it.

And as with your automobile, preventive maintenance is key.

Changing your kid's oil every 3,000 miles is a good start.

Just like cars have gauges to let you know your fluid levels (brake fluid, gasoline, automatic transmission, windshield wiper, Diet Coke, and so on), so do kids. Men don't really have to actually look at the gauges in cars. Men know, inherently, how many miles before you run out of gas, whether you're going to need to change the oil this weekend, that the windshield fluid has only four or maybe five shpritzes left.

This is how women are with their children.

It's been 45 minutes since he had that graham cracker; time for cheese! Wait, why are you giving him that slice of bread, he needs protein! He's 15 minutes past nap time, this is a problem, hand me that cookie—good for seven minutes, but then watch out! Better have the orange juice ready for when he crashes, which will be right as we enter the shoe store! Wait—I see there are two apple slices left in this Ziploc—he didn't finish the apple slices? Quick! To the cereal bar, and step on it!

You just need to watch your kid's gauges. How long since he ate? Slept? Peed? Bit somebody? By feeding, resting, potty-running, or amusing him before he hits the redline, you can usually avoid having to call a tow truck. (And, of course, watch out for the beans, or he'll never pass the emissions test.)

Q: Did you really need to include that last fart joke?

Madam, I told you, there are some things you just will never understand.

Q: It takes my kid forever to do anything—put on his shoes, pick a flavor of ice cream, get out of the car, walk down an aisle of the supermarket. It's very frustrating. How can I make him move faster?

Well, I guess you could start by completing the grand unification theory to reconcile relativity and quantum mechanics (hint: the answer seems to have something to do with supergravity, string theory, or tiny particles called—I kid you not—p-branes. You may write your own joke here).

Once you have mastered grand unification, or so the theory goes, you will be able to control time.

Until then, however, you'll just have to chill out.

Truth of the matter is, children are like time themselves: You cannot make them move faster or slower (attending a lecture on grand unification theory may make time *seem* to go slower, but this is only an illusion). In just the last week, I have heard actual dads in actual supermarkets, ice cream parlors, and the like utter the following phrases:

"If you would listen more, this would be a lot easier!"

"If you don't choose which ice cream you want you're not getting any!"

"Why can't you walk without touching everything? Is that so hard?"

The response, if their children were able to verbalize it, should have been thus:

"Father, you are mistaking me for a fully sentient being, capable of rational thought. Clearly, my recently developed verbal skills, coupled with my appearance having taken on a more normally proportioned human shape, has led you to this erroneous conclusion. I assure you that, while the particular lunacy of my recent youth has waned, I am still quite incapable of anywhere near the degree of controlled behavior you are seeking. Would that it were so; but the grievous truth of the matter is that I will remain thoroughly inexpert in these affairs for quite some time, emerging from this embarrassingly inept phase just in time to enter puberty, when I will exchange my incapacities for something more fitting, such as morose resentment. So enjoy this while ya got it, bub. This is as good as it gets."

Q: **My kid likes to argue. About everything.**

Sorry, sir, that is not a question.

Q: **My kid likes to argue? About everything?**

Better.

Arguing is to a four-year-old what hand-wringing is to a Democrat. It's just a natural state they fall into. Just this morning, I had the following conversation with Max.

"Max, we're outta bagels. Can I make you a sandwich for lunch?"

"Dad, what's a router bagel?"

"Ha ha. No, Max, I said we're OUTTA bagels."

"No you didn't! You said router bagel! I heard you!"

"Max, I promise, I did not say router bagel. I said we're Out, Of, Bagels."

"You are wrong! Because I heard you! You said router bagel! What's a router bagel?"

"I'm sorry Max. You're right. I said router bagel. I'm sorry. I didn't mean that. I meant to say that we're out of bagels. I didn't mean to say router bagel."

"What's a router bagel?"

"I swear that I do not know."

"Then why did you say it?"

It happens like that all day long. "Dad, it's twenty o'clock, time for cookies." "No, Max, remember, see, we talked about this, the big hand is straight up, and the little hand is on the five, so it's five o'clock, see? Straight up means o'clock, and the other hand. . . ." "It's twenty o'clock! You don't know because you were in the other room when it was twenty o'clock, but it's a good thing I was there, so I know what time it is, but you don't."

You can't argue with logic like that. You can only hope to distract.

"Max, let's put on your shoes."

"No shoes today! It's barefoot day. Today is Tuesday, and Tuesday is barefoot day."

"Max, look! I bought cookies!"

Turns out, if you give a kid two cookies, he will hold one in each hand, keeping him busy enough that when you're putting on his shoes he will not hit you.

Q: I am a single mother, and after I stopped breast-feeding, my breasts never returned to their normal size. Can you please inspect them for me and make sure they're all right?

Yes, as the author of a parenting book, I feel quite expert in this matter. I would be glad to.

Q: My boy hits me a lot. Other than trying to keep cookies in his hands at all times, is there anything else I can do?

Unfortunately, most doctors will not perform sex change operations on four-year-olds, so you're stuck with the reality that, at this age, girls turn into, well, girls, and boys turn into, well, short samurai.

Here's what apparently happened: When God was passing out testosterone, there was a typo in the instruction manual. "Vait, vait, testosterone at four? Can't be possible. Should be fourteen. I'll have to call de manufacturer. Oy, vell, dat's vat the book says. Okeh dokeh, boys, have fun! Zap!"

And with that, four-year-old boys developed the following conversational ploy:

"Good morning, Max."

"Punch in the arm."

"Ow! That hurt Daddy. Don't do that."

"Punch in the stomach."

"Max, you are going to have a time out if you hit Daddy any more."

"Head butt in the stomach. Go ahead, do what you must. I am just following my star."

The oddest variation is this: I will go into Max's room when he wakes up in the morning, and as usual, we have a few minutes of cuddle time before we start our day. I use the term "cuddle time" anachronistically, because Max does not actually "cuddle" any more so much as "pummel." I will lie next to him, my head buried softly in Mister Dolphin, trying to catch a few more seconds of sleep, while Max, mindlessly, aimlessly, repetitively, hits me in the back. I hardly notice this anymore; as far as I'm concerned, this is close enough to a cuddle. I can usually sleep through it.

Suddenly, the pummeling stops. Behind my back, Max has stood up. Like a professional veteran of the WWE (that's what used to be the WWF, the World Wrestling Federation, but had to change its name to World Wrestling Entertainment. The World Wildlife Fund sued them for using the acronym WWF—and won! It was the greatest victory of the wimps over the bullies since *Revenge of the Nerds II*. By the way, it's not called the World Wildlife Fund anymore. It's just WWF. The nerds must have thought that was cooler. Once a nerd, always a nerd, you know)—anyway, like a professional veteran of the WWE, Max leaps high, obtains a sitting position *in the air*, and lands on my back.

"OOF," says Daddy.

"Oy!" says Max.

But that's not the killer part. Here's the killer part:

Max starts to cry.

"Daddy, you hurt me! Your back hurt my bottom! Owwwww!"

As I noted a moment ago, arguing is futile. Resistance is futile. I apologized for hurting his bottom with my back, as I recently apologized for hurting his fist with my hard jaw. Max, sobbing, socks me one, just for good measure.

My advice in this matter: Keep your distance, and protect the family jewels at all times.

Q: **Who put the bomp in the bomp-ba-bomp-ba-bomp?**

Turns out it was this guy, Jerry, in 1956. He heard some guys standing on a corner under a streetlight singing, "ba, ba," and he said, "You know, I think something's missing."

Q: **I'd like to shake his hand. He made my baby fall in love with me.**

Some women are easier than others. I'll pass along your request.

Q: **I will be spending an entire day with my four-year-old this weekend. What should I do?**

It is best, I have found, to leave your brain in the shower in the morning. This will prepare you for a day with a four-year-old.

I don't know why so many dads think they'll be able to relate to their kid so much better once the kid starts talking. I think dads forget that once they start talking, you have to start listening, which, with a four-year-old, is very much like watching soccer. Once or twice a game an actual goal is scored, but for the most part, there's just a lot of running around that doesn't lead to anything.

Max has moments of great insight—"I'm a boy and Quinn's a girl and boys like cool stuff and girls like pretty stuff"—and moments of great tenderness—"Daddy, you are a good daddy, so you get 21 kisses!"—and moments of great humor. "Oy! I fell down and said, 'Oy!' That's funny! Whoever says 'Oy!' the most is the funniest." (This is the truest statement about comedy I have ever heard.)

But he, and all of his kind, have an astounding ability to beat a good thing to death. If you grab him around the tummy and he laughs, you must continue this at least until next Tuesday. If you close your eyes and he runs behind you, and you say, "Where is Max? Where did he go?" and then you spin around and find him, and feign astonishment—well, this is so hysterical, you must repeat it for at least a month. Inevitably, you will tire of these games, and he will not, and somebody will break down in tears over this conflict. (That's usually me, but not always).

So, waking up stupid helps.

Speaking of stupid: At this age, you will be tempted to purchase board games for your child, because you have some idyllic image of afternoons spent playing Monopoly in rapt pursuit of Park Place and Boardwalk (a loser's strategy, by the way. Too expensive and landed on relatively infrequently. The best strategy is to go for the orange properties—Tennessee, St. James Place, and New York—or the red ones, Illinois, Indiana, and Kentucky. Those get landed on the most. And don't waste your money on railroads. Those are for chumps).

But the board games you play at this age are interminably vapid. The worst of all is Candyland. Basically, whoever gets the Ice Cream Floats card wins the game 19 times out of 20, so what's the point?

So, my advice is, wake up stupid, and avoid board games. Just go where lots of other fathers are (movies, playgrounds, museums; avoid strip clubs at this point) and do what they do.

There is, of course, one other thing, one much, much more important thing, that you can do.

Be there.

That's it: just be there.

You can go to movies, and the park, and the ball game, and Disneyland, and the moon for all it matters, but if you really want to spend the day with your child, just . . .

. . . be there.

Look around, and if you can find a spot on the floor that is not covered with toys, sit on it. Pick up the nearest doll, and say, in your most robotic voice, "I am the doll from the planet Blobby. I have just come to this planet. Can you please tell me what dolls do on your planet?"

Your child will take it from there. All the other dolls, and cars, and balls, and blocks, will be invited to meet and instruct the doll from the planet Blobby.

You should listen. You will learn a few things.

This game may start to pale, for you, in a few minutes. It will not, for your child.

Hang in there.

Dads are used to looking forward, five minutes. We will be happy when the groceries are put away, when this report is filed, when this mess is cleaned up. Your child is trying to teach you what Baba Ram Dass could not. Ram Dass was Richard Alpert, the Harvard professor who got kicked out for experimenting with LSD with Timothy Leary and writing about it. His seminal work, *Be Here Now*, tried to teach a generation about a more simple, spiritual way of life, a way of being in the moment.

Which is exactly what your kid is trying to teach you when he refuses to get out of the bathtub, or get in the car, or end an endless game of Doll from Planet Blobby. Your child is in the moment and of the moment. This is why kids both refuse to get into the bathtub, and to get out of it: Why would a dry person want to be wet? Dry is the perfect state. And, later: Why would a wet person want to be dry? Wet is the perfect state.

And, of course, why would I want to stop playing Doll from Planet Blobby? There is no other game. This is the game.

And so, if you can, let your busy mind rest. Breathe deeply of this game. Do the doll's voice, over and over again, and after a while, if you are lucky, you will be allowed to lean over and hug your child, and you may even get 21 kisses. And, as Max did just the other day, he may allow you to take you in his lap, and he may look up at you, and say, "Daddy, pretend I am your baby," and you will rock him, slowly, slowly, and bury your face in his hair, and just for a moment, you will remember that smell, that feel, that impossible closeness that you still carry inside you, the closeness beyond words and before words; behind the hitting and the arguing and the incessant chatter, here, in this very quiet moment, you can find that impossible closeness for one more moment, this very moment, because there is no other moment, only this one, and you may even find yourself singing:

It doesn't matter where you go, or what you do,
I want to spend each moment of the day with you,
'Cause you started something—can't you see?
That ever since we met, you've had a hold on me?
It's crazy, but it's true:
I only want to be with you.

Permissions

"Dancing In the Streets" Words and Music by Marvin Gaye, Ivy Hunter and William Stevenson. © 1964 (Renewed 1992) FCG MUSIC, NMG MUSIC, MGIII MUSIC, JOBETE MUSIC CO., INC. and STONE AGATE MUSIC. All Rights Controlled and Administered by EMI APRIL MUSIC INC. and EMI BLACKWOOD MUSIC INC. on behalf of JOBETE MUSIC CO., INC. and STONE AGATE MUSIC (A Division of JOBETE MUSIC CO., INC.) All Rights Reserved. International Copyright Secured. Used by Permission.

"Happy Together" Words and Music by Garry Bonner and Alan Gordon. Copyright © 1966, 1967 by Alley Music Corp. and Trio Music Company. Copyright Renewed. International Copyright Secured. All Rights Reserved. Used by Permission.

"I Only Want To Be With You" Words and Music by IVOR RAYMONDE and MIKE HAWKER © 1964 (Renewed) CHAPPELL MUSIC, LTD. All Rights Reserved. Used By Permission of ALFRED PUBLISHING CO., INC.

"Yes Sir That's My Baby" Words by GUS KAHN Music by WALTER DONALDSON © 1925 (Renewed) GILBERT KEYES MUSIC

COMPANY and IRVING BERLIN INC. All rights on Behalf of GILBERT KEYES MUSIC COMPANY Administered by WB MUSIC CORP. All Rights Reserved. Used by Permission of ALFRED PUBLISHING CO. INC.

"Father's Day" Copyright © by Songwriters' Guild. Reprinted by permission.

"New Morning" Copyright © 1970 by Big Sky Music. All rights reserved. International copyright secured. Reprinted by permission.

"Time Passes Slowly" Copyright © 1970 by Big Sky Music. All rights reserved. International copyright secured. Reprinted by permission.

"Darling Be Home Soon" Words and Music by John Sebastian. Copyright © 1967 by Alley Music Corp. and Trio Music Company. Copyright Renewed. International Copyright Secured. All Rights Reserved. Used by permission.

"Turn Back the Hands of Time" Words and Music by JACK DANIELS and BONNIE THOMPSON © 1970 JULIO BRIAN MUSIC and JADAN MUSIC CO. All rights assigned to WARNER-TAMERLANE PUBLISHING CORP. All Rights Reserved. Used By Permission of ALFRED PUBLISHING CO., INC.

"Can I Change My Mind" Words and Music by BARRY DESPENZA and CARL WOLFOLK © 1968 (Renewed) WARNER TAMERLANE PUBLISHING CORP. All Rights Reserved. Used By Permission of ALFRED PUBLISHING CO., INC.